The Joseph Communications:

Revelation

Who You Are, Why You're Here

For Joan
without whom none of this would have been possible.

The Joseph Communications:

Revelation

Who You Are, Why You're Here

Michael G. Reccia

Band of Light
INC.

First Paperback Printing: April 2008
Fifth Paperback Printing March 2018

e-Book edition: September 2012

Published by The Band of Light Inc © 2018
1930 Village Center Circle #3-6568
Las Vegas, NV 89134
USA

thejosephcommunications.us

ISBN: 978-1-906625-07-8

Printed in the USA by LSC Communications Inc.
www.lsccom.com

The authors and publisher do not dispense medical advice nor advocate
any technique as a form of treatment for either physical or medical
problems without the advice of a medical practitioner. In the event that you
use any of the information in this book for yourself the authors and the
publisher assume no responsibility for your actions.

Contents

'the Field' and 'the Fall' – a Brief Explanation

If you are new to *the Joseph Communications* and have not read the other books in this series, allow me to qualify the terms 'the Field' and 'the Fall', which Joseph refers to at points throughout this book.

The Field

When referring to 'the Field' Joseph is describing the conscious field of thought-energy we, as spirits on Earth, are surrounded by and live within. Every second of our lives we project our thoughts and beliefs as to the nature of reality into this energy field. The Field is actually created and maintained *by us*, but we have lost sight of this fact. As a result of us forgetting this, which is in itself as a result of 'the Fall' (see below), the Field is not operating as it was originally intended to. It was supposed to serve us, but at the moment we, in effect, serve it. It exhibits, and seeks to perpetuate in us, a negative charge and outlook, and, because of this and its disconnection with God-Light, is maintaining itself and us via a finite and dwindling amount of energy. The Field in its present state, and therefore also we as human beings existing within it, cannot last much longer. Joseph urges us to re-energise the Field with God-Light and, by doing so, to transform it and take control of it once again for the betterment and continuance of mankind and of the planet.

The Fall

...is a term that Joseph applies to a complex decision and action taken by human souls millions of years ago which resulted in a cataclysmic change in vibration that plunged the Earth into a darkness we and the planet are still suffering from and feeling the effects of. This change in vibration separated us in conscious thought from our God-heritage and resulted in the negative, violent, power-hungry world and society we currently live in.

Foreword

Before Michael introduces Joseph I would like to introduce Michael to you. Michael has been a friend and a colleague for many years. We hit it off from the first moment we clapped eyes on each other. Michael had taken it upon himself to edit and produce a magazine in order to support his decision to quit his full time employment and apply himself to being a spirit medium. It must have seemed strange to my then employers (a print company in the North of England) that I should be sharing jokes and chuckling away with one of their clients to the extent that I did after only a few minutes in each other's company. We thoroughly enjoyed working together. I helped Michael produce the graphics for the magazine, but after that first issue the owner placed its artwork and print elsewhere and I didn't think I'd see Michael again. Little did I know…

One day, maybe a year or two later, my wife and I went along to a party at a neighbour's home. Not knowing anyone there apart from our neighbour, and not particularly wishing to go, I probably reluctantly said, 'Yes. Sure. It'll be fun. Let's go.' Once there, we found ourselves in a dimly lit room full of 20 to 30 year olds, mostly from the advertising and sales industries. I really didn't wish to be there and neither did someone else by the look on his face. Sat on a solitary chair amidst everyone else was Michael. He beamed when he saw me and I guess I did the same.

So, we met each other for a second time, and from that point onwards became good friends. We went on to run our own publishing company and for a while Michael put his work as a spirit medium on the back burner. Eventually the company was wound up as a going concern and we both went our own ways – Michael picking up the threads of his spiritual work once again.

It was a couple of years after this that Michael wrote his book *Answering the Questions Mediums are Asked Most* and asked me to produce the artwork. Consequently we discussed other 'little' projects we might undertake together.

Joseph's first book, this book, was one such project and Michael will explain in his introduction how it came about.

I think it's safe to say that when we first started sitting to record Joseph's communications we had no idea of the threshold on which we stood. Since then so much has happened as a consequence of undertaking this work on behalf of Joseph and the myriad souls who, through God, move mountains to make it a reality. A small group has coalesced about Michael, while behind the scenes a huge number of souls work to bring about the publication of this and subsequent titles containing wisdom and guidance from higher orders of existence. They (we) do this out of love – for those who are 'trapped' in an unceasing round of incarnation, continually repeating themselves, enthralled by the glamour of the Earth plane, forgotten to themselves.

There are other groups, other, similar attempts to open the eyes of people across the Earth right now, chipping away until one day each of us opens our heart to God and decides to listen, to recall who or what we are and then to realise it's time to move on, to grow, to evolve spiritually... and to go home.

So, why Michael? Well, his guides once said that they worked with him because of his 'scientific' nature – his impartiality, his ability to try and distance himself from the message and take himself out of the loop. It's not always easy. Some psychics, mediums or channellers, we are told, have their own agenda (quite often with good intentions) and put their own spin on the communication. To avoid this happening Michael almost never reads 'spiritual' texts so that he can never subconsciously 'colour' the communication he channels in light of information he has read. In other words, he takes his task seriously and disciplines himself.

So, why this group, this *Band of Light*, as we have been called? The truth is that, while Michael channels information as accurately as he can, he remains an instrument, often unable to recall what has transpired. This is why he asked me to sit with him. I was there to record Joseph's communications. And, when both of us didn't have the wherewithal to transcribe the recorded sessions onto paper, a way was found, as you'll see in Michael's introduction. In ancient days (and Michael remembers living this way long, long ago in another life) the seer or oracle would be supplied with everything they required in order to function as a messenger; they were not expected to feed and clothe themselves or to work in the field, but simply to communicate with the ancestors, the angels and God. However, in our modern, rush, rush, world this is no longer the case. Most people are too busy to even think of themselves spiritually or find it fanciful that a communion between souls 'on Earth' and in other planes of existence is possible.

So, Jane, Tony and myself are happy to help both Michael and the soul groups behind us deliver *their* message, for as Joseph says, he's only a spokesperson and Michael the instrument.

Whatever your beliefs are, if you only pause to consider the points made in this one book our work will have been worthwhile.

David Openshaw.
September, 2007.

Giving Voice to Joseph – An Introduction

Joan looked sad and troubled.

For seven years I had been lucky enough to learn from this remarkable woman who had become my spiritual teacher. I had met with her each week throughout that time and she had helped me to develop my mediumistic gifts and prepare for the demonstrations, workshops and lectures that were destined to become part of my life, together with the thousands of one-to-one 'readings' I would subsequently conduct, both in my own home and in the homes of those requiring information and reassurance from 'beyond the veil'.

Those seven years were, by this particular evening, a distant memory. As I chatted with her around her cosy fireside I had already worked professionally as a medium, nationally and internationally (via postal readings requested from all over the world), for a number of years. I regarded Joan as one of my closest friends, closer even than family, a member of my soul group, and a dedicated guide and teacher who had always been there for me in challenging times. On this evening, however, it was she who seemed troubled as she recalled a series of events that obviously still caused her pain and which, despite having discussed all aspects of her past with me, she had never once mentioned until now.

Joan had had a close friend, now departed, with whom she had sat for spirit trance communication privately over a considerable period of time. Betty had conscientiously written down the communications that Joan brought through during these sessions in long hand, with Joan remembering little or nothing of what she had said once they were over, relying totally on Betty to record communications that she hoped would one day be made available to a much wider audience. Whilst Joan was in trance a spirit guide, a soul who always appeared to her dressed in a red robe, would speak through my teacher and give the two ladies all manner of information of vital importance to humankind – information concerning who and what we really are and why we are here; information that answered the fundamental spiritual questions each of us asks at some stage during our lives.

It therefore came as a severe blow to Joan when Betty died suddenly. She had lost one of her closest friends and there could not, of course, be any further trance sessions between the two ladies. Thank God Betty had written down the words of the 'Man In Red' with such diligence! Betty might have moved on, but her legacy was still here – a unique and precious record that needed to be preserved and made available at all costs.

Following the service on the day of Betty's funeral Joan politely asked her friend's daughter if she might have the volume she had produced in conjunction with her mother as it was of considerable importance to her. Betty's daughter, a zealous member of a certain religious group, replied that she had read her mother's book, that it was obviously the work of the devil, and that she had, therefore, flung it into the back of the fire where it belonged, happy to have delivered an appropriate fate to such an evil object.

Joan had grieved over the loss of the book and the information it contained ever since that day. As she told me her story for the first time, however, an idea slowly formed in my mind and I began to wonder whether the information the book had contained was truly lost forever. I was an experienced medium, after all, and it had always been my wish to provide mankind with something other than clairvoyant messages from family members; something lasting that could be accessed by future generations, which is why I had insisted on incorporating workshops and lectures into a work quota that had for many years heavily featured the intimate clairvoyant readings and public 'message' demonstrations people inevitably wished me to provide for them.

What if *I* could sit to re-contact and record communications from 'The Man In Red'? ...Why not? I wasn't a trance medium at that time (that ability would develop later, and was destined to play a major part in the transmission of further books in the series) but I saw no reason why the communications could not be accessed *clairvoyantly* – that is, with me listening to what the spirit had to say and passing on his message to someone else whilst in conscious control of my mental faculties. It was as though an unseen someone was prompting me to consider this at that moment, and there and then I suggested to Joan that I was willing to put in the time to see if I could make it happen. Joan was most enthusiastic and said we should begin sitting together soon. I, however, had a definite feeling that instead of working with her on this project, as I would usually have done without question, I should this time sit with my close friend, business partner and fellow spiritual seeker David, who had expressed a desire to join me in a meaningful spiritual endeavour for some time.

David was as enthusiastic about the possibility of bringing through something of real worth to people as I was and, despite our hectic individual work schedules at that time, schedules which would become ever more demanding as the months and years went by, we set aside an initial afternoon to see what would happen.

At the time David worked from home in an attic room, which contained the computers and related equipment he was expert at programming and operating. We climbed the little ladder into the roof space, set up a cassette tape recorder (how times have changed!), switched off the lights and withdrew from this world into the peace of a spiritual meditation. I instantly became aware of someone drawing very close to me from the spiritual dimensions, a gentleman surrounded by a glowing aura of red energy who wished to speak to me, and so, having first prayed that all communication that might come to us that afternoon would arrive via Divine will and approval, I surrendered my senses to this spirit as much as I was able to and began to bring through a stream of information.

Twenty minutes later, exhausted, disorientated, but also exhilarated, I slowly returned my senses to this physical world and David and I found we had successfully taped a first short 'bulletin from beyond', which David immediately copied to his computer, also burning it onto a couple of CDs so that we each had a copy. No way would the information be lost or destroyed this time around!

In subsequent months and years we met as regularly as time allowed to communicate with 'The Man In Red' as we called him. We tried to adhere to a pre-arranged schedule, we really did, but the communications, which gradually became lengthier, needed, of necessity, to fall in with our heavy workloads, and there were inevitably times when either or both of us couldn't make our other-worldly appointments. We did succeed in meeting on a number of occasions, however, each time gathering more astounding information from 'The Man In Red'. We knew that this should eventually be collected into a book, but could not imagine how this was ever going to happen as neither of us had the time to transcribe our discarnate visitor's words... and a book is an expensive undertaking. We were advised from the spiritual dimensions, however, that we needn't worry and that we should keep the faith and continue to bring through the information. A way would be found, we were assured.

Some three years after we had made that initial link with 'The Man In Red' there came a pivotal point which changed things forever, and which can be summed up in three little words.

I met Jane.

Jane is, quite literally, my 'other half', a term I do not use lightly or flippantly, and one which has become increasingly significant and relevant as the years since we first became a couple physically have unfolded. Jane had also been a long-time seeker of spiritual enlightenment, and almost from the moment we got together our individual goals fused into one. We attended demonstrations and held workshops together. We sat together to help people visiting our home, Jane giving me additional energy to aid the delivery of accurate one-to-one clairvoyant communication. Further, Jane now also began to sit with David and myself for subsequent communication sessions, the addition of her energies to our little group allowing 'The Man In Red' to deliver even longer addresses whenever the three of us met, with myself as the mediumistic channel for his words.

At this point, and after all this time, we were finally given a name... 'The Man In Red' introduced himself, and would henceforth be known as...

Joseph.

Furthermore, this elevated and enthusiastic spirit who, to my psychic eyes, had previously only been visible as an indistinct red glow on the periphery of my vision, suddenly coalesced into sharp focus, taking on the far more aesthetically pleasing form of a not-too-tall, finely-boned man who appeared to be in his mid-fifties, and who sported a neatly trimmed little beard, twinkling eyes and a nifty choice in tunics. We subsequently learned that Joseph was not, in fact, the same communicator from those original sessions Joan had held, and that he and I had a unique and delicate spiritual connection that had been patiently waiting in the wings since my birth for the moment when it could be activated to allow his crucial messages to be delivered. Joan's mention of the lost book and her sadness at this turn of events had been the spiritually-planned catalyst that would galvanise me into action and activate the series of events that would lead to this information being made available to the world. Joseph's red hue, so similar to that of Joan's original communicator, was also explained, as you will discover when reading this book.

The material expression of the group's spiritual intentions, which included plans for additional books, websites, CDs, podcasts, etc. continued to gather pace. Jane's employer at that time – Peter – had also examined various spiritual philosophies, and Jane felt he might like to listen to Joseph's recordings. His reaction upon hearing them was overwhelmingly positive and enthusiastic. Like us, he recognised that these sessions simply had to be made available to a greater audience and he instantly set about the meticulous transcription of the communications onto his computer – a huge task that would take weeks to complete.

Soon it became apparent that we had collected sufficient material for a book – actually the first of what would become, at the time of updating this introduction, *five* volumes by Joseph with a sixth in progress. The material chess game we witnessed play itself out around us in order to give us the means and the time to publish Joseph's first book is a story that could fill a volume in itself. It is not my intention to go into the complex and often miraculous details of what happened here. I will simply say that heaven, Earth and numerous mountains were moved in order to make available the title you are holding, during which period David, Jane and myself increasingly experienced a unique harmony of purpose between us and formed *the Band of Light*, a name Joseph suggested we might like to adopt for our group, in order to make more information available to the world through a variety of media.

So, here you have it – *Revelation: Who You Are; Why You're Here,* the first book in the *Joseph Communications* series, in which Joseph speaks of life, death, the universe and, well, yes… *everything.* Preparing this title for an e-book format (did I mention that times had changed?) plus further hard copy printings also gave us the opportunity to at last include a further chapter – *Positive and Negative* – that had not appeared in the first imprint but which was very obviously intended by Joseph to be an integral part of *Revelation. Positive and Negative* had 'fallen through the net', as it were, due to the demanding and diverse material commitments we had at the time, almost all of which have now been abandoned to allow us to dedicate as much of our remaining time here as we can to making Joseph's words available to an ever-expanding audience.

Where relevant, the communications are preceded by my notes, which chronicle our progress from those initial sessions between David and myself to my meeting with Jane and the eventual formation of *the Band Of Light*, and also give a little background information on each session.

The notes are not important, however.

Joseph's message *is*.

Much of the material these pages contain may come as a surprise to you on one level, but should also resonate with your soul on another. If you feel as though you recognise the concepts Joseph is putting forward in some way you have to remember that, on a soul level, *you already know them*. Joseph is simply putting you back in touch with yourself, reminding you of them so that you can bring a new power and understanding into your own life, into the lives of those around you, and into the lives of the billions of souls – men, women and children – around this globe for whom life desperately needs to change for the better…

…Today.

Michael G. Reccia.
Revised introduction, Summer 2014.

An Introduction by Joseph

I have waited for many years to find a suitable outlet for my thoughts, but you must understand that they are not just *my* thoughts; they are the thoughts and the beliefs of the many souls who inhabit the sphere, the area of illusion, the projection (for all energy allows the projection of illusions) that I live in. They are the thoughts of many souls, put together for the purposes of wakening the 'sleepers'.

The book ahead of you is supposed to disturb you. If it disturbs you, this is good. If you put it away then you are not yet ready for its message. This book is designed to inspire you, to trouble you and to make you look at the inner world (which is your *real* world, rather than the outer world you have bought into) in a different way.

My name is *Joseph*.

I have lived on your Earth many times. It is also my Earth, of course. I have been in the spirit realms for many, many years – for centuries, for thousands of years. I chose at one point not to come back to the Earth plane. It was difficult because there were many things I enjoyed there. I enjoyed food. I enjoyed grapes. I enjoyed wine. I enjoyed having ladies around me. I enjoyed sunsets. I enjoyed the beautiful vistas I saw from my bedroom window when I was a citizen of Atlantis. But something made me turn my back on the Earth plane…

It was pointed out to me that there were other mountains to climb, other vistas to look at, and I decided to travel onwards rather than return to what I was convinced was an illusion. It was pointed out to me that there were many things wrong with the Earth plane and that souls were returning there for the wrong reasons; that they were not learning; that they had become trapped in a cycle of existence and had made gods of things that weren't God – things that didn't matter. They had turned their backs on the *true* God …**the God that was within them.**

Many of Earth's religions had also done this, so that they were, in effect, praying to themselves and instructing their devotees to pray to the priests and to the holy men. A few on Earth understood that they were part of an illusion and a few rose to great spiritual understanding, but *even they* chose to come back and not always because they wanted to teach – often it was because they wanted to be adored, and that, too, is a trap. All power comes from the Source, not from the individual. The aggrandisement of the individual draws its energies from the negative side of life and is a channelling of the negative side of life. People who truly work spiritually work in the quiet, work without thought of their own egos and work in order to go on working for the Light when they pass beyond this illusion, not so that they can come back to Earth and repeat the process and have people bow down in front of them.

Our group's intention with this book is to turn things on their heads and to bring an argument for Light into the darkness.

To demand nothing.

To dictate nothing.

To say: 'Here is the book. It is your right to read it. It is your right not to read it. It is your right to reject it. It is your right to accept it – in whole or in part. We advise you to read it, we want you to read it and we invite those of you who do so to become workers for Light and truth because of what the book says to you.'

Things must change.

Let that be your motto; let that be your daily outlook on life.

Things must change.

Things cannot continue in your world as they are. You are still killing each other, you are strangling the planet, and you are ignoring your spirituality – your Source. You are 'dreamers' and you don't know it. You are tied into the dream to the extent that you have forgotten your heritage.

You are told in many of your religions that the way to God is through the holy men and the priests. This is nonsense! **The way to God is through your own heart.** You are a 'god' in the making – you are a child of God, which is what Jesus said to you, which is what many of the prophets have said to you, but you have given exclusivity to them; you worship them as saints and they never wanted you to. They said, 'Here is the way, here is the truth, here is the Light' ...and, instead of taking on board the message, *you worshipped the messenger.*

This is not necessary. Worship no one, only Creation. Worship what is *within* you – the one, true God, the Source of your life and your consciousness, and help to make a difference in this world.

I was not always a spiritual man. I, as much as any other soul, went through lifetimes when I was not aware that I was a soul; lifetimes in which I viewed the universe from the standpoint of individuality and believed it to be so; lifetimes when I thought I was at the whim of a cruel universe; lifetimes when I looked in a mirror and actually believed that what I saw was truly me.

Then, through experience and through promptings (because I was psychic I could hear the voices and could see the faces of people who had gone beyond the illusion) it slowly occurred to me that I was more than this temple of flesh, that I was a spirit, that I was eternal and that I was more than the illusion I was witnessing.

I was also taught that I was creating, that I was adding to that illusion, that I was a god in the making, that I could influence my environment – influence my immediate environment (the environment of my body) and then influence the world around me. I was shown that *my view of the world contributed to how that world was*; that I wasn't at the whim of every storm and tempest; that there was no unforgiving God but God was a constant presence of Light within me and, if I wanted to fulfil my mission as a soul, all I had to do was to spread that Light outwards.

When I arrived in the spirit realms, and as I climbed the spiritual ladder, as it were, many things were revealed to me. I looked in the records of the passage of time for the Earth and discovered many things about its origins. I spoke with angels on the spirit side of life. I spoke with truly wise men and women whom I did not have to seek out but who instantly stood in front of me the minute I asked my questions. I was made aware of the origins of Creation, the reasons for the Earth being there and the nature of man and of his soul.

All these questions cannot be answered in one book. You may not like some of my answers but all I can say to you is that, with my hand on my spiritual heart at my centre, I have researched, tried and tested and believed every word I have given to you. I am not an agent for darkness; I am working for the Light, and it is my intention to give you some indication of your abilities as a child of God. I ask you to test and to prove for yourself everything that I have said to you, and if you find me lacking in any area then reject what I have said.

There will be other books to follow; there are more complex issues that I and others on my side wish to talk to you about. I hope that you will enjoy this one, read the others and support this series of books. Remember that in buying a book such as this you are parting with illusion, nothing more, and you are being given knowledge you will take in and which will change you and change your viewpoint *forever.* I know that every one of you that buys this book will be recompensed. If you find it interesting, pass on the information to the next soul. Give them the book, get them to get in touch with its publishers and spread the word.

May God bless and keep you forever.

Joseph.

Chapter One
Beginnings

Michael's observations: My memory of this first communication between Joseph, myself and David is of a private clairvoyant 'session' one afternoon that proved to be quite difficult in terms of my maintaining a link with the communicator. Joseph had never spoken to and through me before, and there were many pauses in the speech and much grunting, groaning and sighing (which, mercifully, has been taken out of the transcript!) as I struggled to align my vibrational rate with that of this new communicator – 'The Man in Red' as we called him in those early days, due to the fact that he always came through to us at that time dressed in a fiery red robe or surrounded by a cloak of red spiritual light. I was extremely tired and disorientated following this initial session, which took place in David's attic with the lights turned off and with David instigating and monitoring the recording of the session. Subsequent communications became much easier, with far more of Joseph's personality and gesticulations being evident during the periods he used me as an instrument. He has a forceful and demonstrative personality, and would sometimes bang the desk with my fist – not in anger, but to emphasise a point – or wildly gesticulate as he sought to explain certain concepts to us.

When David and I sat for this initial communication we had no idea that the information from this and subsequent meetings would eventually build into a book, although we knew *even at this stage* that the lectures and the knowledge they offered were not simply for us and that it was essential that they somehow be made available to a wider audience. Neither did we know that we would eventually be joined by the third member of our earthly 'team', my partner Jane, and that we would subsequently sit as a trio to bring through Joseph's later communications and much spiritual information from other guides. Any slight repetition by Joseph concerning the themes he wishes to speak about here is due to the newness of our 'connection' at that time, and subsequent talks flow far more smoothly, as you will discover in the course of reading this book, with the communication being sustainable for increasing amounts of time as Joseph and I become used to working with each other.

Joseph: I wish to speak to you about *January*, about the beginning of things, and so I am bringing into your minds a concept that you are familiar with at the beginning of each year, because I wish to talk about a beginning: the beginning of a communication between our level of existence – which is not a level you have encountered before – and yours. By this I mean that this instrument [*reference to Michael*] has not until now been in touch with the group of souls who are today attempting to communicate with you.

I am their 'spokesperson' if you like – it is as good a term as any, although there is no difference or hierarchy between us *here*. The red vibration I bring with me is not my natural hue; it is a beam of energy that is needed to punch through the density of thought that surrounds the Earth plane, especially at this time.

The red vibration is energy to contra the energy of the Earth plane. This instrument [*Michael*] knows that the red vibration is used in spiritual healing to stimulate the physical body and the nervous system in one who has become depleted. However, it is necessary for us, in communicating with you, to build a 'wall', as it were, using the red vibration to keep out the ether from around the true beam of light we are bringing to you, and through which we are able to communicate with you. Were you to see this red beam from our point of view it would look like a tunnel, although a tunnel is perhaps a bad analogy as it has no dimensional width at all, yet we have to try and convey ideas to you using terms with which you are familiar. We are no more than a molecule's width away from you but we have to penetrate your dark level of consciousness in order to speak to you.

What should we speak about? We wish to talk about *beginnings* today, and about the seed that is within the human soul; for the soul is not the seed, it is a covering or vehicle for the seed and not the seed itself. The seed is separate and comes into being of its own volition. Yet there is a paradox here because it does not have that volition until it becomes separate. So, we ask you to consider that God *wishes* separation in order to grow. The volition first comes from God but, at that point, the seed becomes aware of its own purpose. In other words, God at first thinks of separation and, at that point, the separation exists. Again, the paradox is that the separation is a concept of God and, therefore, a part of God, so actual separation never – in terms of your understanding – exists.

So, each seed is separate and yet contained within the Whole that is God, but God allows the seed to experience growth through the illusion of individuality. The seed is then clothed in various radiations that allow it to interact on a physical level *with* that physical level. These can be compared to 'skins' or fields of various energies that complete the illusion of separateness from God. From the inner to the outer, the skins become more dense, but they are nothing more than 'shades' put around a 'light' and, within those shades – and particularly within the outermost three – the earthly perceptions and consciousness reside, but these are nothing more than an illusion or a field which is tissue-thin.

What we are saying is that everything you perceive to be dense, permanent, vast and 'real' is contained within these three outer skins or fields, and that these are permeable, which is why we are able to contact you from our level of 'reality', *which is also a projection* (although a less dense one) that is around the seed that is always a part of God.

This is what is meant by: 'In the beginning was the Word'. In the beginning was the *concept*, and the concept was *separation* in order to *experience*. Following separation, there is growth of what is perceived as the 'individual'. And the amazing thing is that the field energies that lie within the three outer skins are shared by all beings on Earth, *but the field energies are all there is – there is nothing else on this level* of *consciousness*. The level itself does not exist ...only the *perception* of it, as shared by the consciousness of all living things. This is the true nature of creation on your level. So, everything is contained within the individual and the individual is contained within God.

Therefore, all projections by the consciousness into the perceived field energies within the three skins are **dominated by mind, not by substance.** It is the mind that creates and manipulates the field energies; it is the mind that creates the illusion of separation, and it is the mind that presently fills the fields with the darkness we have to penetrate from within in order to reach you.

We are trying to dispel the concept of God as being 'outside' of this physical universe ...or above it ...or below it ...or separate from it because, in actual fact, the physical universe only exists as a field of consciousness, created by God as the individual rather than God as the Whole. In other words, the seed was made 'flesh' and the seed required substance around it in order to interact with itself. And so the consciousness from the seed created the fields. It is God-consciousness, yes, but God-consciousness given to the seed to do whatever it wishes with and to create whatever it feels it needs to create in order to express itself.

Often the 'seed' or individual cries out to God in prayer to help it in areas that God has not consciously created, but which the seed, the individual, has created. This does not mean that the seed is separated from God, but, rather, that the seed has been given God-power to create whatever it perceives to be true, which we hope goes a little way towards helping you to understand why there is such chaos within these three perceived fields. Because the seed, although not separate, has lost its memory of where it began and, in doing so, has allied itself with the fields of perception rather than with its *true* heritage.

Our task in contacting you is to peel back the layers of misconception that separate the seed from its greater Whole and, in doing so, to create an increase of God-power within the fields so that the growth that is expected of the seed by God in projecting Itself into individuality can take place.

We have to warn mankind that this expected growth is not taking place at this time.

The individual is taking part as a player in the same 'play' – is playing and replaying the *same* play again and again without understanding why it is here. And the souls who are being born back into this illusion of individuality time and again are causing their reincarnations on Earth by their *own desire*, and not by any volition on the part of God for them to return to this planet.

Therefore, many souls are choosing to reincarnate into the same conditions they left when they passed on [*into the spirit worlds*] in order to replay exactly the same type of experiences they crave, and that is not the purpose of the three fields. The purpose of the three fields is to allow expansion of God-consciousness, to bring the seed to a point where it becomes more than the seed and can produce seeds of its own. It is no coincidence that reproduction on your level within the three fields is a matter of the seed issuing from the seed. It is exactly the same process on a God-level, with the expectation for the seed being that it bring through further seed, allowing growth of the original seed and the God from which it came.

This is not taking place, however, and because God does not oppose God – how could God oppose Himself/Itself? There can only be gentle direction given from our point of view, rather than coercion. Whilst the seed involves itself in the illusion to the extent that all else is unimportant, the Source can do nothing until such time as, via instruction, the seed loosens its grip on perceived reality and reaches *within* to perceive absolute reality, not the projection.

This is why this communication is taking place and we hope that what is said today gives you some measure of the severity of the situation and the need for perception from within to take place within the seed.

This is why I am speaking to you and this is why I begin our communications with the terms *January* and *Beginnings*. This is how each of you began. This is who you are. We have worked to broaden your [*Michael and David's*] perception to this point – a point at which we can begin to commune with you for the greater good. It has taken three years of organisation by us in order to reach this point, and things from this moment onwards will change in order for the work to be done.

You [*Michael*] will also see my companion, who mostly works, from the point of view of your psychic vision, in shadow so do not be alarmed if you perceive his presence as a shadow or a feeling that someone is intensely interested in what you are doing. He protects me as I speak to you and pulls my consciousness back should the density of vibration around the connection of this communication prove too much for me.

I look forward to subsequent meetings.

God bless All, and may the Light be with you until our next meeting.

Chapter Two
Creation

Michael's observations: Here is Joseph's second talk, given around Christmas time. This second 'connection' was much easier on me mentally and physically. It was as though a lot of work and adjustment had taken place behind the scenes since we last 'sat' for communication, and that the slight problems in achieving vibrational compatibility apparent in that first session had been tweaked somewhat to allow me to tune in more fully and successfully to Joseph's personality. The second paragraph of Joseph's talk on creation introduces the first of his blockbuster statements. Joseph pulls no punches when putting his message across, and there would be many more such thought-provoking words to challenge the way we approach life in subsequent talks, as you will discover...

Joseph: I wish to continue from the point at which we left you last time, and to talk about *creation*; not Creation on a universal level, but creation on an individual level, *because creation is misunderstood by mankind.*

Everything that exists does not exist.

Now, *there* is a statement! *Everything that exists does not exist* ...at least not in a solidified form independent of observation. What I mean by that is that nothing outside the energy Field created by humankind and the individual fields created by humankind exists *independently* of those fields.

As an example, a rock exists as a rock only because the Field *believes* that it exists, and it is no more permanent than the thoughts that have been put into it that give it weight and form within the Field.

Each human being has a field around them. It is often described as the aura, but it is much more than that. The aura, often referred to, is simply a reflection of the electro-magnetic tendencies within and exhibited by a soul, a measure of that soul's health, evolution and spiritual understanding. The soul may be measured by the information which the aura contains – information that can be seen plainly from outside the field, but not from within it, usually, except by psychics and those who are mediumistic, and by what you would describe as shamans and mystics.

However, the aura is only part of the field that is generated by the individual. The aura is the energy field that is closest to the soul and extends for about three metres out from the physical body, with the most luminous and, therefore, the most easily observed part of the aura being at a distance of about a third of a metre out from the body. Beyond this there extends a second field that is linked to the mental process of the individual, and it is this field that allows form to be brought forth.

You might say: 'Well, if I want to create something, I first have to get the materials, and I have to use my hands, my mind and my heart and put part of myself into this creation then I have something that is outside of myself.' That is not strictly true. The object you desire to create already exists within the field *as soon as it is imagined*. It is the need to make sense of the object on a physical level that requires energy to be expended on a physical level in order to see the object. I know this is a complex concept.

What I am saying is that each object created is created *first* within the field without use of hands, tools, or expenditure of physical energy. It is created the moment that it is dreamt of. The field, if you like, is a 'field of dreams'. (*Michael speaking*: at this point I can see Joseph is smiling because he is showing me an image of the film *Field Of Dreams*... so he has a sense of humour.) It is a field within which the individual dreams up everything that it needs. The images within the field are then rationalised within the greater Field, which is the Field of mankind. In other words, the thoughts appear to be more solid and manifest themselves within the greater Field of mankind.

Therefore the phrase 'be careful what you wish for' is a very apt one indeed, because what you wish for or dream about you create within your own personal field, and it manifests itself and is contained within your own personal field for a time. Then it manifests itself, to a greater or lesser degree, in the circumstances around you, which are created by the Field of mankind as a whole. This takes time, dependent upon the individual and the individual's belief (i.e. strength) in being able to dream, create, and manifest what it wishes for. The mental field of the typical individual, however, is filled with so much heaviness, so much disbelief and so much dross that it takes a great deal of mental power and time (as you measure it) for the dreams to manifest themselves around the individual.

It is important that you understand that things are not meant to be this way. The God-essence or manifestation of God that the individual actually *is*, is able to instantly project within the field of dreaming whatever it conjures up, whatever it perceives, and that is how the individual is *supposed to* manifest experience on this level. But, over the centuries, this ability to believe in creation coming from the mind and the heart rather than the hands has been lost. The Ancients knew that creation was not a matter of taking up tools; it was a matter of sitting and seeing and projecting and always believing, because it is that belief that solidifies the images within the Field.

What I am saying is – and this can be very dangerous – **it is possible for you as individuals to have everything and anything that you desire in the measure that you believe in what you are creating.**

...But you do not believe this. You believe that the Field humanity gives out is 'reality'. You believe that you are separated from the things that are around you. You believe that you have no connection with the things that affect on you on a day-to-day basis. You believe that they are random forces, that you are at the whim of some vengeful God, perhaps, and that you are a 'boat' buffeted on a sea of chance and circumstance *...and that is completely untrue.*

Every object and every situation that manifests in a life has been created through mental energy and first activated by the soul that those circumstances are happening to. And it is in

God's image that you are made in that you are a 'Creator', every minute and every day of your existence, within the greater Field, you are a Creator. You have been given God-power – you need never fear for want of any object or fear any loss or lack, because there can be no lack as long as you create supply. YOU create supply. You say it is God who has created supply, and in the greater sense it is, but the manifestation of supply comes when you believe in yourself as being God.

I am talking, of course, about positive manifestations, but the Field of humankind at present is set to manifestations of a negative nature. It is set to despondency. It is set to violence. It is set to a compulsive acquisition of other objects within the greater Field. How nonsensical this is from our point of view, when anything that you desire you create within your own field. There is nothing for you as an individual outside of that field except a field of reference – the greater Field of humanity, within which you experience the situations you have created for your own growth. The mind is a tool with which to create what you need around you in order to grow, **and no object has any worth except as a tool in order for you to grow.**

To say *you cannot take it with you* is a fallacy. You take it *all* with you when you come back home to the spirit worlds because it is all within the field you have created, but you take the purest form of that which you have created with you, not the actual solidification of the situations that you are growing from, but the *essence* of those tools. That is what you take with you. (*Michael*: I'm sorry, I don't understand that...)

...Each situation around you is a manifestation of the deepest desires of your own soul to grow, whether that situation brings you pain or loss or struggle or challenge, it is a manifestation from yourself that you have decided you need. When you retreat from the field into the greater vibrations, within your aura are contained the results of the thoughts that you have brought forth in order to grow. For example, if you create an apple, you take the *results* of having created an apple back with you into the greater vibrations and not the physical manifestations of the apple that present themselves within the greater Field of humanity. You take the results or the *consequences* of having created the apple. These are what you take with you.

So, you can never lose anything because, from cradle to grave, within the greater Field of humanity everything is contained within the aura of the individual that pertains to that individual's growth as a soul. There is no 'reality'... *There is no reality* – there is only perception and through the mind you set up certain shadow plays that you involve yourself in, in order to become more God-like, but that is all they are – shadows. You are projecting part of yourself, and the situations around you are part of yourself solidified, projected through the physical mind, in order that you may perceive different aspects of yourself and grow as a result of that.

We will speak on another occasion about 'realities' that are withdrawn from the Field of humanity, the *greater realities* if you like, but at present we wish to give a greater understanding of the nature of so-called 'physical reality'.

Everything comes from nothing. Men study the universe and say, 'How could it come from nothing?' but everything comes from nothing because there is nothing except the 'Essence'. And the Essence projects in order to further Itself, to become more than Itself, to grow... yes, even at God-level.

What we are trying to bring to humanity is an understanding that the Field is able to be manipulated by the individual, that no prayer is wasted, that no striving for Light is a nonsense, because every thought has equal creative power and **every thought** *manifests*.

The troubles you find yourself in presently exist because the individual and the Field choose to manifest the worst aspects of themselves. Souls on Earth say they want things to change, and yet we find such difficulty in persuading individuals to give some of their time in thinking of the Light, in bringing into reality the Light through their mental process and changing the bias of the Field from self-seeking negativity to a more enlightened and creative (in the spiritual sense) society.

That is our task, and in order to implement that task we have to first bring the individual back to the basics, and tell you that *you are everything* – everything that you perceive, because it has all proceeded from you, just as you have proceeded from God. And once that is all stripped away – the mistaken concept that we are placed into a fixed world, and that we are temporary, when in fact it is quite the opposite... *we* are fixed and the *Field* is temporary and malleable – then we can begin to do work, then we can start to heal the Field, start to repair minds and also to move souls away from the Field so that other souls who have not yet incarnated can be born into this particular reality.

We appreciate your endeavours and we would leave you with the thought, during your festivities, that the greatest gift we can give you is the realisation that you are everything and that everything proceeds from you. If you want health, you create it. If you want wealth, you create it. If you want harmony, you create it. And, in doing so, you begin to influence the greater Field, which is our intent in bringing through this information. We intend it to be distributed into the Field and not to be hidden.

Chapter Three
The Circle

Joseph: I wish to talk with you again today, this being the third part of our conversation concerning the nature of reality. I wish to talk to you about the circle, about the sphere – because, however you proceed outwards from any point on a sphere, you eventually arrive back at that same point – at the starting point. This is what people cannot grasp within a linear universe; they cannot conceive of something that does not begin and does not end, and yet the evidence for this is *everywhere*, at molecular and atomic level, and within nature throughout your world.

I am discussing atomic structure because the nature of the atom is to be spherical, and each atom is re-used. I remind you that you personally [*Michael*] were taught while you were at college that matter cannot be created or destroyed. Now this is not quite true... physical atoms are re-used, re-designated, and they cannot be destroyed due to their being a reflection of God-creation, which is contained within a circular or spherical energy field.

It is the same with life; it is the same with the human cycle. Everything is cyclic... it is supposed to be that way; it is embedded within the nature of what we are. It is God-consciousness and God-consciousness, if you like, is circular. It is cyclic. It brings Itself back to Itself. Therefore, It does not have a beginning. It does not have an end. **It simply IS.** It is self-contained and you are contained within that creative circle (cycle) of the sphere of God-consciousness.

Every life should be regarded as a circle, as a circular motion of the soul that that life is attached to. In order that the soul actually comes back to the point where it began following its incarnation it goes through a cycle of events whilst on Earth that eventually bring it back to itself and return its consciousness to a higher level. So, no journey on Earth, no journey *anywhere*, in fact – no adventure, no setting out – is actually in a straight line. It is a circular event, because it brings back to the soul doing the adventuring, or the 'setting out', the benefits of the encounters that it comes across during each adventure.

The soul does not grow older; the soul cannot grow older because its vibration is circular. The soul maintains itself; it is self-perpetuating; it does not run out of energy. The physical journey is, similarly, a circular event with the physical body that is attached to the soul undertaking the series of adventures that begin with it being created, being formed around the incarnating soul and then, later, the body returns to the circle of energy it has come from, both on a spiritual level and on a physical level. It is the same for us in our sphere of consciousness. We are aware that we are simply adding to ourselves by the endeavours we undertake. We do not 'go away' from anything 'towards' something else. We do not journey outwards. We are simply embarking on a further circular vibration that will bring benefits to us, so that our being, our essence, may be enriched by the experiences we absorb while passing through and reacting with certain circular wavelengths. All life, all situations, are wavelengths of the soul and, as the motion of those wavelengths unfolds in a circle, certain things happen along those energy vibrations.

In reality there are no births and no deaths; there are simply points of observation from within that circular motion, and the consciousness of the soul is also taken on a circular motion. So, nothing you perceive of as lost is ever lost; nothing you perceive of as having been damaged is, in truth, damaged. What you are observing is simply a bending of a particular wavelength in order to bring to the soul certain perceptions, certain experiences that eventually enhance the wavelength that is returning the soul to its original point of consciousness. The soul 'arrives' back at its original point of consciousness without damage, but it is enriched by the experiences it has encountered via the changes to the wavelengths that have taken place during its circular journey of existence.

The soul, in effect, does not travel anywhere. The soul, from the point of view of your earthly perception, is born into your level of consciousness, grows physically and mentally through a certain number of years and then comes back to its spiritual home. In reality it goes nowhere. **None of us ever go anywhere because everywhere is within us** – this is what I am trying to get across to you by talking about circular motion. You are self-contained within the self-containment that is God. You cannot go anywhere. You only perceive movement, which is actually the change of the wavelengths that you are experiencing, in order to bring your consciousness around to a more complete vision of who you are.

Therefore, you should take heart with regard to your perceptions of people having been lost, having been damaged, having been tortured, having been hurt. In fact they haven't been; they have simply been viewed as such from one point on their circular journey of consciousness. When they get back to the start point that damage is seen for what it was... simply an illusion that has been used to enrich their sense of being by bringing to them – and the people whose lives they have touched along that journey of consciousness – more understanding of themselves and the universe around them.

And you may say: 'Well, how can they receive more understanding through being damaged, or tormented, or tortured, or murdered, or maimed?' You have to understand that the circular motion of one soul, at certain points, touches the circular motions of the souls around it and, in doing so, that journey of consciousness takes on for a time (and it is only for a time) certain vibrations from the souls who touch that circle. In these circumstances it often seems that the less advanced soul has taken advantage of the consciousness of the more advanced soul, and this is because you are looking at things only from the point of view of your circular journey across the Earth plane. In fact, the consequences of an advanced soul touching the journey, the motion, of a less advanced soul far outweighs the consequences of a less advanced soul touching the path of a more advanced soul.

In other words, on a level of soul-consciousness, the soul whom you perceive as having been murdered, or maimed, or tortured, or lost *knows that no harm has really come to it*. It knows that it has simply passed through an energy field during which time its vibrations have touched the vibrations of another soul in order to donate Light to that other soul; in order to donate to that other soul a point of consciousness upon the other soul's journey that illuminates a part of its journey.

So, you have to look at the seemingly negative things that happen on your plane as being *in soul-reality* moments when some Light has been put into the darkness; although you will say, 'The murderer is still a murderer', or, 'The torturer is still a torturer', or that people have 'got away with' this or with that. No. What has happened in these circumstances is that – whether the other soul is conscious of it or not – some Light from the advanced soul has been donated to the journey of the soul who is not yet so advanced, so that that soul can consider that illumination during what you would term a future point in that soul's circular journey, and take it on board in free will. Take it on board and, hopefully, realise that there is a lighter, more uplifting way to live. In effect, the soul who has been – from your point of view – murdered or tortured has elected at an advanced level for those things to happen to it in order that it may donate some Light to the path of the darker or less enlightened souls whose circular journeys it touches during that conjunction of wavelengths.

We [*Joseph and his colleagues*] are also on a circular journey – it is no different for us, except we are *aware* of the fact. The circle of our level of existence has to touch the aura of the communicator [*Michael*] in order that our consciousness – our intent made known through a sharing of consciousness – can be passed on to your level of consciousness. It is the same thing. Michael and myself are touching at a point along our separate wavelengths so that I can donate something to this level of consciousness through the consciousness of this soul [*Michael*] who is touching my wavelength. And so it is with all souls.

45

No one is ever lost, no person is ever murdered, no person ever dies in tragic circumstances *because you cannot die.* You have moved only in consciousness, only in terms of a wavelength, away from your original state, and the soul is just passing through that period. Once it comes back to the spirit worlds, once it completes the circle, it realises this and is released from the effects that seemingly negative period had on that point of the circle of experience.

This is why you 'sit' on Earth in [*spiritual*] circles. This is why there is power in circles, because you are joining together the circular wavelengths of a number of souls in order to create a passageway for vibrations, which is also circular. The nature of God is circular. Words do not do justice to what I am trying to say, but *God is a circle.* Life is a circle and the building blocks of life are circular by design. The atom recreates itself because it comes back to its point of starting out on its journey of physical existence. This is why matter can be re-dedicated by what you would call Higher Authority, by God-authority. An atom can be re-designated as it sets out in consciousness – because all matter is alive – it can be re-designated as part of another object, but that other object, that new object, is also a circle – *another circle.* This is why things return to dust on your level of existence, because they are completing the circle of their current existence in form and are returning to the essence they were in consciousness before they were designated as a certain circular wavelength that you perceived as an object for a short period of time.

You see, it is no coincidence that the seers on your level have used crystal balls because the sphere or circle enables those who are spiritually aware, and who have opened up their vibrations somewhat to the greater reality, to see other points on the circle *through* a circle. This is how the 'future', as you understand it, can be seen 'ahead of schedule'. The seer on this level is seeing into the circular motion of the soul that he is sitting with, or sitting on behalf of, and can see more points on that individual's circle than the sitter himself or herself can.

I have spoken for long enough and I do not wish to tire the communicator, but I wish you to know that I am more heavily involved in your lives than you perceive, and I am working with a purpose to enable God's work to be done through yourselves. May God's Love be with you until the circular wavelength of our meetings comes back to the point at which we meet.

Chapter Four
Death and Karma

Michael's observations: This would prove to be Joseph's most shocking meeting with us to date, and not entirely because of the subject matter, although that, as always, brought its own revelations. You see, on this occasion Joseph was not alone, and had brought a very special 'guest' with him... I have witnessed many things clairvoyantly during my years working as a medium – angels; advanced souls who are so refined spiritually that they appear to be made from light itself; thought forms; rather less advanced souls who can best be described in their current state as beings of darkness... but never, until we sat on this particular afternoon, had I come face to face with a 'man' from another planet (outside of a science fiction film, that is). But there he was, as clear as day, standing in front of me for a few moments, with, behind him, a vision of the massive and beautiful world that he inhabited. It was quite a unique moment, as you can imagine. I had been aware for some time of the fact that the whole universe, being a part of God, was alive, and that there just had to be souls living in physical bodies on other worlds, but to actually meet one, however briefly, was both an honour and a humbling experience.

Joseph's dot-within-a-circle reference was also something of great significance. I purposely avoid reading anything by other mediums or mystics, or any spiritual or scientific books – the reason being that I don't want to subconsciously colour or influence any information that comes through me from the spirit worlds. I want each message received to be as true to its source material as it possibly can be. It was, therefore, very satisfying to discover, after Joseph's fourth message session, that David, who has studied esoteric literature extensively, had come across the symbol before, and that there were many other references to the dot within a circle image from other spiritual writers and inspirers.

Joseph also demonstrated during this session that he knows of some of the spiritual discussions we have had at times when we have not been aware of his presence. It appears that he is constantly linked to our vibrations on some casual level and is able to tune into David and myself more specifically whenever he picks up something of relevance to the topics he wishes to present to mankind.

Joseph: I wish to talk about *death* this afternoon. The people of Earth see death as a finality and not as a transition – that much you know, but I would like you to look at death in a different way from today, because death is an *escape* from a set of vibrations that have been put into motion around the soul on Earth.

When a soul is born and takes the journey through the Earth life it is surrounded by a 'bubble', an egg, a circle or sphere of energy that accompanies the soul throughout its earthly life, and that sphere of energy has built into it a certain number of sub-energies that come into play at specific times during the soul's life. Each one of those sub-energies envelops the soul in certain circumstances that must play out in order that the soul might grow. And these sub-energies are attached to the vibration of the human body, not to the actual soul. The soul is enveloped in the energies, but it is the human body that is needed to link the soul to the situations that are contained within the energy sphere and will play out at certain times during the soul's life on Earth.

The body is the conduit, and when the physical body is shed the set of vibrations – that 'bubble' that surrounds the soul – is also shed, freeing the soul. So, death on a physical level is so much more than simply relinquishing the body to the Earth; it is the conclusion of a series of events, and that – after all – is what the earthly life really is, a series of events that play out around the soul whilst it is 'travelling' through the physical plane.

I would also like to try and make you understand that the events that surround the soul, that are linked to the physical body, are linked *to that one body*, and for that reason it is questionable as to whether your medical science should allow sections taken from one body to be placed into another, because along with the section of the body that is transferred from one physical body to another, there is attached to that section an interplay of vibrations that relate to the original soul only. And, therefore, when we talk about the body being the 'Temple of the Soul', we mean that each body is a *unique* temple of the soul it houses. It is not meant for anyone else. Its vibrations are meant for that one individual soul and, in your terms, are tailored and engineered to the karmic needs of that individual soul and to no other soul.

So, it is questionable as to whether transference of body parts from one soul to another should take place, and it is a greater degree of understanding into the sources of disease that is required rather than transference of parts from a seemingly healthy body into another body that is diseased in the hope of effecting a cure.

The interplay of vibrations when body parts are transferred can cause havoc around the soul that is receiving those parts, and can also – to the extent that the donor body is mixed with and linked to the new body – affect the karma of the soul receiving the new body parts. The specific and unique nature of the energy bubble that relates to each body should be respected and understood. Transference of body parts is dangerous, as the karmic energies designed for one body are capable of partial transference to another body. This is why physical death is necessary, to free the soul from the situations it has chosen to go through in order to grow, and also for the physical body to be transferred back into its elemental condition, so that it can be neutralised by the Earth, and then brought forth as another body without having an attachment to prior karmic vibrations via the bubble it was previously linked to.

Am I making myself clear? David... am I making myself clear? [*David indicates that he understands what Joseph is saying.*] I know that this is the first time I have spoken to you directly, but it is possible for me to do so and, as we hold subsequent sessions, I will invite discussion, once we have the basics of what it is I wish to bring through to you in place.

So, to return to the subject of death – of course there is no death of the actual soul, but 'death' occurs on a daily basis for each soul everywhere, because the vibrations of that day are let go of, are relinquished, and so it is with physical death. It is simply a relinquishing or a letting go of vibrations that are no longer of use to the 'travelling' soul.

Now the question of release from karma is an interesting one. The karma of the soul that has been on Earth can still have an effect when the vehicle – the physical vehicle and the vibrational sphere attached to it – have been let go of, but the soul *is* allowed a period of refreshment and rest during which there is the absolute bliss of being released from the work – and it *is* work – of having had to go through a series of karmic events as a result of choosing to re-enter the physicality of the Earth plane. And the soul feels lighter; the soul is returned for a time to a contemplative state of being where it is free from having to make any karmic moves. And it is, during that time, able at its own leisure and pace to contemplate what happens next.

It then is assigned – if it decides to return to the Earth, to a further physical existence – outfitted, as it were, with a karmic bubble that will affix itself to its new physical body, and both are brought forth from the subtle energies of the universe by the *Lords of Karma* – who do, in fact, exist. You could describe them as 'Elders' who have in their charge the wellbeing of the souls under them.

There is a hierarchy to the Lords of Karma, as with everything else on the spirit side of life. There is an evolution, and it is decided, at many levels that extend right to the Godhead, what is best for each soul in accordance with that soul's desires and free will. That information is then transferred and diluted through various levels of consciousness; through various workers who have the karmic interests of the human race and the individual soul at heart. Then, at its 'lowest level' (as you would understand it) the Lords of Karma call the soul into another chapter of its evolution. This is both chosen and accepted willingly by the soul, and the process is carried out according to a timescale that is up to the soul and up to the Lords of Karma in charge of the evolution of that soul, and up to the Godhead.

If a soul decides that it does not wish to visit the Earth again it has to have an anchor in some perceived reality, and so it will be called from the state of contemplation that it is in to exist, to interact, with one of the spirit worlds, and will be seen in a 'body' that it is comfortable with; and in many cases will have no conscious memory of having been released for a time to recuperate and gather strength for the next stage of its journey.

You can liken the process to reporting back to a central point on the progress you have made during your time in a particular existence, of which there are many. There are many physical existences that are open to the evolving God-child, and not all of them are on this world, on this planet. There are other opportunities on other spheres that are in a physical universe that are open to the God-child if it wishes to take them up, and none of them deal with karma in quite the same way that it applies to souls on Earth. I noticed you recently talking about the seemingly brutal nature of nature in this world – and I have to tell you that your situation on Earth is somewhat unique, as you will learn in future communications, and that karma on Earth has a particular 'twist' to it for reasons I will explain in a future book once I have laid the foundations of spiritual knowledge out for the reader. Some of the opportunities on other spheres involve the soul in incarnating into an advanced society, where the challenges are on a mental plane, are on a scientific plane, yet still involve working hand in hand with God-knowledge.

The scientists on certain worlds, in certain societies, are not as blocked to inspiration and to the acknowledgement of a greater life and a greater consciousness as they are on this particular world. So, there are wonderful opportunities, where science and progression on a material level are concerned, for the evolving soul. But each of them involves that soul being incarnated into a denser matter to some extent and, therefore, taking on a physical body – and taking on as an addition to that physical body a set of circumstances that they have to play out, always within a sphere, in order to evolve through that particular chapter of their infinite existence.

There is, were you able to see it with spiritual eyes, a planet within this solar system that has been uplifted beyond the vibration of physical eyes, which exists relatively close to the Earth, between the Earth and Mars. The planet is about three times the size of the Earth. There is life on that planet, and it amuses us when you look for evidence of life within the universe and it is right on your doorstep; and it amuses us that you are observed 'through a glass darkly' – that is, without any knowledge of it taking place, by this other world.

[*Michael*: He's withdrawn for a moment because he's brought in one of the people who live there to show me what they're like. I'm looking at a tall person – humanoid but tall – very thin. I can't really see their face. It's as though I'm not supposed to see it, but I can see somehow a male vibration – tall – I would say six or seven feet tall – and very thin, very ethereal looking, because they're not weighed down by the same measure of gravity that we have in this world.]

They, too, come to an end in that form. Everything within the *physical* universe 'dies' because it is cyclic, and the whole universe is experiencing, (I noticed you writing something about karma this week) the whole universe is experiencing a karmic growth... and the whole universe – because it is contained within the mind of God, because it is contained within a circle – is infinite. It does not have corners or edges as some of your scientists think it does. It is a cycle of karmic energy relating to the souls who live within it; and it will come to an end, but the souls within that cycle of karmic energy will not, because they are infinite and the karmic energy is only a temporary construct around the souls at the heart of it, that allows them to perceive and to grow.

So, death is bound up with karma. It is necessary because of karma, because – if I can make this link – karma and 'life' and 'death' are of the same thing. You cannot extricate one from the other, because karma only applies to the cycle of energy and evolution that is put around a soul, or around a physical area of being. So in that sense it is purely an energy and does not exist as, of course, I explained to you in an earlier conversation – nothing really exists.

So, to 'die' is to do nothing more than take off a certain 'suit of clothes' and to experience the freedom of the Godhead. You may ask why a soul needs to go through this constant experience of 'life' and 'death' and moving on. Because the universe, because God, seeks to be more than He is. The perfection of God is absolute, but perfection is not something that stands still. Perfection evolves just as everything else does, and it is the wish of God to send forth vibrations of Himself and to set in motion circumstances that allow those vibrations to become more than they were when they were first created. And because the souls that those vibrations represent are a part of the Divine, it follows that, as they evolve, to some extent the Divine also evolves; the Divine becomes more, the Divine finds more expression, moves forward. The rate of vibration of the

Godhead becomes even finer because of the endeavours of the God-children sent into matter, who are constantly evolving and bringing back a refinement to the Godhead.

And – this is amusing – all of this happens without anything ever moving, or going anywhere. It happens around the souls, but the souls do not travel. A soul does not travel from birth to death. A soul merely is immersed in the bubble of karmic energies around it, which play out around it. It goes nowhere. It changes its vibrationary rate because of the things that happen to it, the things that are *really* happening to it vibrationally... which brings us back to the dream and the dreamer, and the power of the soul.

The next phase of evolution on your planet is to begin harnessing the power of thought for good and, through scientific means, to harness the power of thought to construct and to heal. There will be scientific proof and a movement towards that event within sixty years. There will be great leaps forward in the understanding of the unseen.

I have 'died' many times, as you would understand the term. I have died many times, and, for example, was alive on your world in the area of Australia before the civilisation of aboriginals was even there, when the landmass was joined to another area of land by a bridge. Quite a huge bridge of land, and one of my first – I can now remember it, I could not for some time – one of my first incarnations was as a person in that environment, long before your world had any technology. And it was a charming time, because the race of people I belonged to had no fear of death and were childlike in their acceptance of the wonder of Creation around them. They, too, were dreamers, and were so in touch with their God because the generations of human mind had not yet placed barriers between God and the individualisation of the soul and they could bring forth whatever they dreamed of. And so life was very pleasant for us because we simply dreamt up and would have communal dreams of what we needed. These would then manifest themselves in the landscape and the environment around us.

I know you have been asking who I am, and when there is time I will build up a picture of what my life has been like. One of my earliest recollections that I can now access – because I have looked into the book of my life – is of that time. And death was a simple affair; it was not something that we feared. We regarded it as a circle, and we used to draw a circle in the sand with a point in the middle of the circle, and that was our symbol for the universe; that was our symbol for creation. Unknowingly it was also a symbol for karma, with the point in the middle of the circle being the soul, and the circle itself being the bubble of consciousness and vibration that surrounds the soul in order that karma might take place.

I will try and give you – as we proceed – various symbols and explain their meaning to you as time goes on.

We have already talked of the cyclic, the circular nature of God. One of the earliest symbols of man on this planet was the dot within the circle, and that is what it means. But, of course, we also understood from the great teaching of this very simple symbol that the circle revolves and the dot stays in one place. It stays in one point, is immovable, is unchanged by the circling of the energies around it. The dot doesn't go anywhere... as you get closer to the centre there is no movement, as you go further away from the centre there is the illusion of movement by dint of your being out on the edges of vibration as it were; further from the Godhead.

I feel that I have spoken for long enough today. I wanted you to look at death in a different way; because my purpose in all of these conversations is to present things in a different way, to build up an alternative picture of the universe for you. Having dealt with the incarnations of souls, it seemed only logical to deal with the *transitions* of souls which, of course, only take place in terms of vibration and not of movement.

It's funny, isn't it, that your society picks up psychically (whether it is aware of it or not) the symbols that have been around since the beginning of consciousness in your world? What do you put into the earth with your dead (as you would call them) but wreaths, which are circular?

And so, with that image of the circle again, I will leave you and God Bless you. Mindful of the circle being an image of the course of your lives, it is inevitable that your lives and mine will touch again at this point on the circle. I thank you for your endeavours.

Chapter Five
Needs

Joseph: I want to talk to you today about expression, and about how solidification comes to concepts out of nothingness, and about how the soul constantly creates and recreates a framework within which it can operate.

As I have said to you before, nothing that exists *exists*. From the sea of consciousness each soul, moment by moment, decides what it will create and, at that moment of decision, vibrations of construction surround the field that the soul exists within (the field of vibration you would know as the aura or the 'egg of being', within which lies the consciousness, the essence of the soul).

As the soul dreams up an image of what it requires, that image is created around the soul by the wishes of the soul's mind acting upon the receptive molecules that surround that soul on a physical level of existence. Those molecules are – from that time onwards – linked to the soul. So, if I said to you, 'You can create a chair,' you can, but creating a chair also creates consequences. You cannot create a chair without having consequences, because the image of the chair is linked to you. So the effect of creating a chair will last in your consciousness long after you have discarded the actual chair. You see, you will have put into being a series of events. You will have said, 'I am going to create a chair,' and the chair is then created and is linked to you because you created it. Therefore the effect or consequence of having created a chair, will be with you long after you have forgotten that you ever created the chair.

Of course, I am not really talking about creating furniture. I am talking about creating *consequences in life* and this is what the soul forgets when it incarnates into the world of matter – that whatever it creates *has consequences*, has ramifications, has restrictive or constructive forces that come with that choice of creation and which impinge upon the soul or uplift the soul long after the physical object itself or the set of circumstances have been created.

Therefore, everyone on Earth should choose very carefully indeed what they create minute by minute or day by day. Of course they do not realise or accept that they create everything with their minds, yet they feel it is perfectly acceptable to create seemingly 'outside' of themselves... I was with you watching the footage of the car-plant and looking at the robots creating cars. [*Michael: both David and myself had, prior to this session, been watching television footage of robots making cars.*] We accept that, 'outside' of ourselves, if we apply sweat and time to something, we can create it on a physical level, but we do not accept that we create things – we actually create *everything* – from within ourselves merely by thinking. It's all right to say,

'Outside of myself a car is created,' but not to say, 'I have created that vehicle or had some hand in creating that vehicle by my wishes or by my acceptance of society as it is.'

If we take the example of the car, mankind will create cars for a limited amount of time because you accept that you require cars at this stage of your evolution and progress. But then some inspired person will think of a better alternative and at that point everyone will buy into that better alternative or want to create that better alternative. So, your cars will be replaced by something else, not because you have gone out into the world and created that alternative *physically*, but because you first had an inspiration and that inspiration spread like a thought-virus to other people, who said, 'Yes, that is a good idea. We will now adopt this system of transport rather than the one we had before.'

Every concept, every product, every state of creation you see around you is created not actually in or from hard matter, it is created from the mind and then given form by the fields around the souls that thought-create such objects, solidifying those objects into an acceptable form for themselves and for the rest of the souls living in a material world.

The reason I am talking to you about the concept of creating form is to get through, not to you who already know this [*Michael: i.e. – myself and David and, later, also Jane.*] but to you who will eventually read this, the importance of your choices of thought on a daily basis; because the soul so often creates need where it needs nothing.

Need is an illusion, which is also a relevant topic given your enterprise on behalf of the spirit and on behalf of God at the moment [*Michael: Joseph is here referring to our wondering how, with a limited budget at the time, we would ever publish his communications*]. There is no need – and the pun here is intentional – there is no need to need, because *there is no need.* Souls on Earth create need as a concept and therefore *bring it into being.*

Society is spending a lot of time at present considering and studying the health of souls. In this area, however, there is a major lesson that you have yet to learn and it is this – *you are creating a need outside yourselves for health.* You do not believe that you are healthy; you do not believe that you are perfect. You create a need outside of yourselves and say, 'I will be healthy when I have gone to this doctor, or to that hospital, or when I have taken that drug, or attended that course, or investigated certain things that must be wrong with me.' And hundreds of millions of souls believe this and, therefore, create that need outside of themselves, and then they cry to God, 'Father, we have a need for health.' Well, yes, you have a need for health *because you have created it.* There is no need. Need is just an example of the soul encased in a Field of heavy matter thinking itself into a situation where it believes it has needs outside of itself.

My purpose in talking to you today is to tell you that there is no need outside of yourself for anything...*no need outside of yourself for anything...* and yet souls tie themselves into a life that is full of need; full of objects outside of themselves, which they chase after having first created them.

It may surprise you to be told that illness is created as a desire of the soul. How can this be? How can anyone desire to be ill? But they do... because they desire attention; they desire love; they desire to go through a process in which people are taking care of them; they desire to give in to the overwhelming belief that at some stage in their lives they will be ill. They desire that process because practically every other soul does; they buy into the co-creation of so many souls and desire to be a part of it. Then, when they *are* a part of it, they are terrified as to how they can get out of it. And they can get out of it by simply realising that there is no need, there is no illness, there is no imbalance except that which is created by the soul, and just as the soul can turn on any method, object or situation creatively, simply by thinking about it ...*so it can turn it off.*

If your soul is ill, turn off the illness. If your soul is poor, turn off the poverty. Turn on a different set of values. The values are only there and the ability to create is only there to allow the soul to grow. Instead, at the moment, mankind is mired in creating negative fields around itself which it thrives on, which it loves, which it has given God-power to. Everything comes forth through the use or misuse of God-power ...and the expectations today of so many souls on your planet are of illness, grief, pain and suffering when it needn't be so.

I wish to say to those of you reading this that if you *truly* don't want to be ill; if you *truly* want to be rich; if you *truly* want to be free; if you *truly* want to be loved – create not a need but an acceptance, create a remembrance of what you *already have*. You are already loved. You are already perfect. You are already wealthy. You are already included in Infinity. It cannot be otherwise. And yet you choose to separate yourself from these things, and the world will never become the better place to live in that so many people hope for until sufficient numbers of you start to create in thought daily – to visualise, build, and see the place you want existing *now*.

Concerning the field of each soul, if you could see the auras of many people, you would see that they expand outwards from their bodies for *miles* because they feel they have to include within them the car; they have to include within them the holiday; they have to include within them the friends; they have to include within them the clothes; they have to include within them the shops. And so they expand their auras to take in and link their spirit to all of these physical things, and daily they create that need which expends energy and makes them less than they should be as spirits, and which defeats the object of them being on Earth, which is to create something positive; to become aware of their God-properties.

God does not want you to create anything negative except that you learn from having done so. God wishes always for the soul to remember *Who It Is* and to bring forth God-properties, God-traits, God-power, God-energy.

This is how we glorify God – by bringing forth Light, simply by *knowing*. Worshipping is knowing. Worshipping is saying: 'I am God; I am good; there is nothing else outside of myself or within myself and each day I bring forth Light. Each day I need only look inwards to find everything that I need. Each day I create positive things, things for the glory of God.'

And this is what your doctors should be doing, looking at their patients and refraining from saying, 'I see illness.' Instead they should be looking at their patients and saying, 'I see an imbalance in the way you are thinking which I can rectify by loving you.' *Now there's a revolution* – and this is what you should expect from your doctors. This is what doctors should expect from themselves. Instead they treat meat; they treat bones; and meat and bones are just a projection from the soul and not the soul itself.

Your politicians should sit *to see good*, to send out good, and we look forward to a time, *which will come* when you will have councils on Earth which sit regularly, not to govern and to guide but simply to *be*, and to bring through into this world Light and harmony. These are the people you will vote for, not because of transient policies that affect the material, but because these people will be in tune with the God-within and will be able to change the world by sitting on behalf of its peoples, who will also be drawn into a time when they sit to create good – good for themselves, good for others, good that will radiate out from this planet and, as you would describe it, will 'Christ' this planet. They will bring forth a Christ-Light – and we do not talk here of Christ the individual, we talk of the power that flows through the individual – they will Christ this planet and raise it in vibration so that it will become part of the community that includes the worlds we talked about last time, and these worlds will become visible to you because the whole Earth will have become so spiritually accomplished – so spiritually elegant.

So, my task today is to point out, again, that everything is created by the soul, and I also want to return to the beginning of our conversation, with regard for the need for choices to be made carefully, because the situations you build into your lives on this level, once created, you find hard to un-create, and the soul each day of its life should be free to create a whole new set of circumstances. It is not, however, because, to return to the example of the chair, the chair comes with a whole set of consequences. The chair has attached to it a whole set of vibrations that you have created; and even when the chair is not there, the consequences of creating that chair are still with the soul.

So it is with the worry and the pain and the anger you bring into your lives each day. **You cannot be angry today without**

reaping the consequences of that anger tomorrow. And the situations you create as souls actually band around you like the skins of an onion, and slow down the progress of your soul because it cannot see the Light due to the heaviness it has placed around itself. It is essential that each soul – on a weekly basis would be ideal – sits quietly and lets go of the creations it no longer needs: creations of anger against people that it no longer needs; creations of pain that it no longer needs to hold onto; creations of upset; creations of greed; creations of jealousy. All of these things it no longer needs it should sweep out on a weekly basis – much as you would delete those contents of a computer you no longer have use for – it should sweep out the things it no longer needs and 'un-create', if you will, demolish and take away from itself that which it no longer needs. Then the soul is free to create purely and this is why some people seem capable of building so much more than others. Many souls, however, surround themselves with the past, and in doing so they cast a shadow over their futures; they restrict their futures.

The soul is a creative force, a creative vibration, and the soul needs to start from the beginning each day. Souls should understand that each day they awaken to is a beginning and that beginning should not be flavoured by the events of the past. Yes, they should learn from their past experiences, but each day should be a new dawn and a new opportunity to create that which is good, that which is positive; and to revel in the fact that each day is eternal and that this life is an opportunity to create. As you rightly said, David, each soul exists as a part of God *right now* and does not have to wait to die to be returned to that source. All each soul is experiencing on the Earth plane is a bubble of reality that is created around itself and that exists within the greater bubble of reality that the whole of mankind is creating constantly.

How much *more* souls would accomplish on Earth if there was no fear of death! You would be amazed at how great a percentage of mankind is held back simply by fear of death, 'What is the point of trying now, I'm too old? What is the point of going into this project because I will not see it out?' And that is a belief, that is a negative creation, something that slows the soul down and makes it so much less capable of doing what it originally intended to do. You not only take yourself with you when you die, you take with you the vibrations that are around you and the projects that you are interested in.

How cruel would it be of Creation to cut you off from the things that you want to do! You are a free spirit, so those projects you put your heart and soul into on Earth have some counterpart on a higher vibration and you will be allowed – to the extent that you have not held yourself back via the vibrations you have created around yourself during your outward journey – you will be allowed to continue those projects, but with greater vitality, with greater insight, with greater love of creation. So, people should live not as though they are going to die, but as though they are going to *live*. And they should live each day, and create each day, and bring Light into each day. Souls are not brought here to be asleep, but that is how they approach this life. They do not appreciate the textures, the substances, the sounds, the sights of this level of vibration because they are mired in their own creations from the past. They are tied down by the 'chairs' they created years ago.

I tell you this to bring you freedom. There is no death; there is no birth; there is simply a change of state in the vibrational rate of the soul so that the soul might grow. And we work to bring harmony to this level of consciousness, but our efforts are diminished because the Light that we are able to create on our level of consciousness has first to penetrate the darkness of this life. And the level of vibration is not *inherently* dark, but has been imbued with that quality by the souls living in it. And, if you will, there was once an 'Eden' for this Earth, there once was a time when, although it was a physical plane, it was remarkable in its beauty. And there were people who lived at that time who had no concept of death, who celebrated a person's passing as part of their life and did not see themselves as separate from that person from that time onwards, knowing in full consciousness that they were always joined to that person, and there was communion with spiritual vibrations, with higher vibrations at that time.

Souls have lost their way, and the souls who repeatedly request and, therefore, experience reincarnation on this level think that they have found Heaven, but they have only found a jail of *their own making*. The soul is supposed to pass through this level, not to repeatedly visit it and repeatedly be encased within it. There are beauties beyond, there are opportunities beyond, a 'breath of fresh air' beyond that millions of souls don't want to take. And it is our mission to bring freedom of knowledge to souls on Earth so that they live each day of their lives to the full, and also to free some of the souls from the constant cycle of reincarnation that they put themselves through, having bought into the illusion to such an extent that they can see nothing else. We weep for them because they believe they are free, yet they are the ones that are cut off from the people who love them on a higher vibration, and there is nothing we can do other than, drip by drip, try to alter their consciousness through information such as the texts I hope to continue to bring to you on a regular basis.

In conclusion, my message today is one of joy, because it says – and this is truth, Brothers – it says there is no death, there is nothing except perfection, and perfection is within you now. It does not even have to be worked at; it just needs to be accepted. It is the *illusion* that needs to be worked at, to be dispelled, to be taken away. Deconstruct your lives is what I say to you. Deconstruct the ideas that hold you spellbound, so that your God takes the place of the 'chair', takes the place of the car, takes the place of the holiday, so that those things are ultimately proven to be empty. Choose to reunite yourself with God – the God-within – and everything else will fall into place.

It bemuses us to have watched the funeral proceedings of the past couple of days, where people dress in black, where people mourn the loss of they know not what. [*Michael: here Joseph is making reference to a funeral that was on the news at the time.*] They mourn they know not what, and they construct around themselves religious ideals that have nothing to do with God, and which restrict them even more. Would that those people put as much energy into deconstructing their beliefs, put as much energy into building a different kind of Earth. We would tell them all to go home, to sit down, to take off their black clothes, to bathe themselves in the colours of God, to bathe their souls in the colours their souls need, because colours are creative... but they do not hear us yet.

Have you any questions, David?

David: No, I need time to digest things first.

There then followed a personal message for David, after which Joseph *broke the connection, concluding his talk.*

Chapter Six
Death Revisited

Michael's observations: During this session Joseph gives us the second of his ancient symbols. In expanding on the theme of death he visited in an earlier session, he once again turns society's thinking about the subject on its head, and also begins to tell us a little about his culture …or, rather, the culture that was a part of one of his many lives spent on Earth. Again, Joseph shows that he has been listening in on conversations between David and myself, referring to our recent thoughts and our discussions concerning spiritual matters at points within the transcript.

Michael begins by passing on Joseph's comments clairvoyantly, initially referring to Joseph in the third person: Joseph tells me he was listening to me say downstairs that God is a Circle (as previously stated, David and myself sat for early sessions in David's attic to communicate with Joseph) and he is saying that death is the end of a *cycle*; and that 'death' is a concept that applies to almost every aspect of life…

From this point Joseph speaks in the first person by 'overshadowing' Michael [*Michael: by 'overshadowing' I am referring to a process whereby he would 'stand' very close to me and 'touch' my aura to enable him to control the communication coming through me to a greater extent without actually taking me into a full trance state – something that would, however, become the norm for our communications as we worked on subsequent books*].

Joseph: Death applies to ideas every bit as much as it applies to physical life. Death also applies to prejudices and to national and international tendencies. Death applies to and is necessary for everything that can be thought of at the point when those manifestations of thinking (those thoughts given mental or physical form) become inappropriate. By 'inappropriate' I mean that, as the spirit or spirits manifesting those thoughts grow out of and away from – grow to be *greater* than – those thoughts, than the eventual potential prison those thoughts and concepts would create were they not to be deconstructed, then those thoughts and concepts have to 'die'.

It is unfortunate that, for many people, 'death' – not only as a physical manifestation, but also as the deconstructor of ideas, of concepts and of outdated phases in life – is something they resist with their whole being, with their whole consciousness. [*Michael: at this point I could feel Joseph rearranging, rethinking his terminology.*]

…Let me turn this around… Death is *life*, because the death of any idea, the death of any person, opens up a stream of changed circumstances – changes that are suddenly open and available to them. **And by immersing yourself in change you immerse yourself in greater life.**

I tell you, many people on your planet are actually 'dead' already. Each day they are dead in that they are living within a personal framework of dead thoughts; they are living within the thought frameworks of concepts they have already outgrown – which they no longer have any use for – and yet they clothe themselves in these thoughts; they continue to believe in them. By night they sleep immersed in them; by day they invest power in them. They continually approach their life from the point of view of things that have already passed.

Letting go is *letting in*. It is the letting in of newness, of the revitalisation that God-energy can bring to us all, yet people are so reticent to let go of *anything*. Death is a cycle. I have died many times. I cannot tell you just how many times because, as I have explained in past conversations, I have incarnated over many thousands of years, and I have, therefore, died many times. And what are those deaths to me today? As I stand here, speaking to you, am I actually *dead*? No, but I am *changed*, and I would not be where I am now had it not been for those deaths. So, death of all things is change in all things and should be welcomed.

You are experiencing problems with religion and with worldwide violence at the moment because old concepts die hard and people invest – the *souls* those people really are – invest a part of their life energy, in thought frameworks, beliefs and ideas that are already dead. If I were to bring a bright light from the spirit world now and place it in front of you, I know that Michael would be able to see it, but if I were to take this same light out onto the streets, no one would see it. They would walk straight through it. If I made it even brighter they would still not see it because they prefer the enveloping 'death' of their old thought frameworks to the spirit truth that could be brought to them today if they would only slough off those thoughts.

So the mission – the mission of missionaries such as Michael and other spiritually alert souls – is to 'kill off' in the people they meet that which is no longer necessary in those lives; to make them aware of the things that need to die in order that they can see the Light that the spiritual messengers bring.

And one day, for each individual soul, that Light must also 'die' to make way for an even greater Light. The souls who pass from your planet are actually not static, not inert, as you know. They progress, and as they do so they continue to experience subtler... 'deaths', if you will, a subtle shedding of the skins that surround the essence that is their soul; and they do this willingly by working to absorb more God-consciousness, by trying to elevate their own consciousness so that they expand their energy field. And in expanding their energy field they are able to take in and appreciate more concepts; more points of view. As we progress as souls through the various fields of being our auras expand to the point where we can fully take in and consider concepts – life experiences – from other souls, and other souls can take in concepts from us. The life experiences remain in the personal histories of the souls who originally underwent them, but the riches in terms of knowledge those souls have gained spiritually by going through those experiences can be shared with other souls, particularly with souls from their own group soul. A point is reached where there is a constant exchange of ideas and of history and experience between souls with a view to those souls determining what they are and what they no longer are at different points in the *now*.

This is why we gravitate towards each other as souls, why we become ever more integrated as we progress spiritually, so that we can share experience and, in oneness of purpose, become ever more aware of the God that we really are. David said downstairs that he feels we never actually reach a total understanding of God, never understand fully what He is – and he is correct [*Michael: Joseph is here making a further reference to the comments that passed between us in the days and hours leading up to this particular session*]. He is correct because the understanding of each soul is always changing and expanding. Because we always are a part of and increasingly contribute to the understanding of the Whole as we progress, integrating our unique experiences into It, the understanding of the Whole constantly changes and expands its nature.

Yet all is contained within the circle I have repeatedly brought to you as a representation of God. So we do not expand *outwards*. We do not, in fact, go anywhere. Rather, through the death of notions and through change, within that circle we become more understanding of the completeness – the wholeness – of the circle which forever contains us, for we are forever within God. It is only thought that takes us 'outside' of God by means of the fields of illusion. We cannot be taken away from that which we already are.

Therefore, when someone dies they do not 'go' anywhere; they are simply shedding a set of outmoded vibrations. They haven't 'gone' anywhere – it is the set of vibrations that has gone somewhere, that has deconstructed, has ceased to encapsulate them and ceased to imprison them.

And any death in the physical is merely the death of a concept, because the physical does not exist; it is only an energy construct that is temporary, and appears to exist because the souls on Earth imbue it with that intense level of 'reality' they immerse themselves in. So, each soul immerses itself in the fields of illusion, yet that illusion and those souls within it are contained forever within God, because there is no separation. It is, therefore, only a matter of taking away – in 'death' – that illusion of separation, so that the soul can see more clearly once again.

All the 'physical' manifestations around souls that seem to cause them such harm are, in fact, mental constructs rather than physical ones, in that they are the illusory products of the creative mind. They are states of being, if you like, not states of mind, although they are first created by mind, but are states of being of the soul that manifest around that soul through the illusion of physical reality, so that the soul can recognise what it is and what it is not. **That is all that spiritual progression is ...recognising what you are and what you are not.** Now, am *I* still progressing? Yes I am, but with a greater degree of my consciousness involved in the process than most souls on Earth are able to apply at this time.

So, when people invest time and energy in material things, in aspects of their lives that they wish with all their will to be rock steady and to be there forever, they are investing their energies into ideas and nothing more. Ghosts and wisps! The physical aspects they see are merely temporary solidifications within the Field of energy around the souls on Earth. They are not real, are nothing more than ideas which are only there to act as tools to aid the soul's progression. **Once man understands this – that his ideas are tools to serve him, to enable him to evolve – then we will be making real progress.**

As I have said before a funeral wreath is a circle, and it was understood by the Ancients that a celebration of death was a celebration of the completion and the conclusion of a set of ideas and nothing more. Forgive my pun – but if people would only try to see life in the round, then we would be able to teach them far more than we are able to at present.

I keep with me – on my level of consciousness – a number of books, and those books *rewrite themselves*. The books are a temporary solidification of my ideas and the ideas of the people who are linked to me within the great group soul that I am a part of; and, as my ideas and the ideas of my brothers and sisters in the group soul are refined, so the books refine and update themselves.

I wish to give you an image of the great group soul of which I am a part – so I am going to compare that great group soul to a galaxy, which you will notice is also round, and despite an apparent constant physical expansion away from its core is actually always spiritually pulling inwards towards its centre. If you ever need to bring to mind an image or symbol of my group soul, then think of your own galaxy. The great spirit-forces of a group soul lie behind the physical manifestation which is a galaxy, and I am, therefore, tying the two images together. As a group soul moves onwards spiritually and old ideas die within that group soul and new ideas are born, so the physical manifestation of that group soul – or, in this case, let us say a galaxy – dies, and is reformed on the physical plane as something else.

So 'death' on your level and 'death' on our level are tied together. Death on your level concerns the death of ideas and the death of circumstances, but we are *all* tied into this process, and the death or letting go of ideas on our level – a higher vibrational level than yours – filters down to your level and eventually causes the death and deconstruction of certain ideas on Earth.

Certain physical manifestations end on your planet and the people of Earth say, 'Why... why has that happened? Why is this thing I relied on so much no longer in place?' Because it is no longer necessary, and the concept behind it that has stretched from our world to filter down and manifest dimly for a time in your world therefore changes – dies – and is replaced by a new one.

Your physical galaxy is a construct, an illusion, simply a physical manifestation of something spiritual, just as the planets are. And it is no coincidence that all of these bodies are circular because they are each a symbol, a bringing forth into matter, an attempt to explain what the illusion is, what lies behind the illusion ...and like everything else they must die and change.

The higher planets on higher levels of evolution also change. They begin to exhibit more Light as they gradually become a purer representation of *That Which Is* behind their creation... God.

So, we have to look in life to death for freedom and for teaching. Death sets you free, and it does not exist. As with everything else I have talked about thus far, it does not exist. All that exists is the sweeping out of old ideas and circumstances so that the soul can move forward via the bringing forth of new ones. The soul does not lose its identity upon 'dying', because its true identity is eternal and has nothing to do with its earthly persona. You are *That Which Is*. The death of ideas – of mere illusions – cannot destroy That Which Is. Cannot harm you. And it is the nature of That Which Is to move on. It cannot be static. It has to grow.

Where do we go? I will talk of that at a later date, within the limits of my understanding, but if I could get past earthly thinking today I would say *welcome death in all things*, in all structures, in all situations. Accept it...

When something goes wrong it does not actually go wrong. The situation simply dies away from you because it has outlived its necessity in your life. In a way you should welcome the end of things, because the end of things heralds the beginnings of other things... it is a cyclic pattern. We understood this as Ancients. It is a cyclic pattern.

The names we gave to people then were indicative of their existence as spirits, and were unlike the single names you give to people now that refer only to this one life. And we talked of people going back to the circle, going back to the sky, going back to the cycle of life, and we believed they would be reborn.

One of our symbols of strength – I suppose you would say of occult strength – was the symbol of fire and flame. Flame was represented as a triangle, which was our geometric representation of that form of energy. I would add to your symbols today – to the one I have already given you of the circle with a point at its centre – the triangle, which is fire and energy.

The Earth is going through what we would describe as a cycle of fire at the moment, a period of fire. Fire consumes. Fire changes. And within your lifetimes you will see what you will consider to be many cataclysms in natural events. But these are simply the deaths of rigid ideas that must go; and when these things happen, try to remember what I have said about them being a part of the fire element at work.

Fire consumes. We used fire to consume the physical bodies of those that had gone on, to consume them because we knew there should not be a link any longer from any soul that had departed back to its physical body. The physical body still holds within it at the point of death concepts it has held to be true during its life, illusions it has clung on to. So, we used the fire element to consume the body totally and then we spoke no more of that individual, but we used the given name to refer to the soul of that person that was now free.

You burn bodies as a matter of storage and space consideration in your funerals and ceremonies today, but you do not understand why fire was originally used; you just have a vague memory of it. Fire was used as a blessing for a departing soul, to finally consume that part which the soul no longer needed.

I bring to you both as I leave you a glass of blue energy, a vessel of blue energy, which you need today. Michael needs it around his head, and David needs it around his chest. There is also silver in that vessel, because both of you are more susceptible to the illusions and pressures of other people than you realise. And I pray that you will feel peace around you this afternoon as we restore you to continue on with your work. Go now and drink, and the energy I have spoken about will be in the water you drink.

There will be more information on elemental symbols and the use of the elements later in our conversations.

Chapter Seven
The Heart

Joseph: Today I wish to talk to about the heart as a symbol and as an action, as a force, and I will begin by telling you that the human body is not put together by accident.

You may believe that the human body has come together through evolution, but it has actually been designed in a very specific way to reflect its 'heart' (if you'll forgive the pun), to reflect its basic elements, to reflect its soul and its link to God.

God can be likened to a 'heart of energy', a centre. We have talked about God as being a circle that emits pulses or cycles of vibration, and it is within these cycles of vibration that we all exist and have our experience.

The human heart is also a centre of energy. The human heart is a reflection, made flesh, of the Nature of God. It is a reflection of the cyclic nature of God-energy and God-consciousness. So little is known about the human heart and the 'heart-centre', as you call it – the energy chakra that lies within the human heart. It is from this chakra, not from the solar plexus, not from the head, nor from any of the other major energy centres, that the being of the soul pervades the physical body.

The seat of intelligence of the soul within the human body is not the head, it is the heart.

And the problem, having witnessed – of course – events that have happened on your level of consciousness over the past fortnight and are set to happen again [*Michael: here Joseph is referring to the London bombings of July, 2005, which had just happened at the time this communication was received*], the problem is that man thinks from the head and not from the heart. This observation has nothing to do with the sentimental or emotional responses usually associated with the heart in that sense.

Man needs a re-seating of the intelligence within the human body from the head – which is merely a calculator – to the heart, which proceeds from the Heart of God.

The human heart is a reflection of the Heart and the Nature of God. The human heart is designed to give out – yes, the blood circulates then comes back into it – but *spiritually* it is designed to give out, out, out, OUT... and the energy it gives out comes from the God-centre.

The heart is trying to teach the soul in human form that the key to existence and harmony lies in *giving out*, an opposite stance to the one your society is taking at present. At the moment society takes in more than it gives out. In the present cycle, in the God-pulse you exist within, society is taking in, wants only for itself, wants only to draw what it wants towards itself, seeks to include everything within its limitations and to exclude everything that is not of itself.

If only society realised that everything is of the self, and that each soul and all souls belong to the Great Self of God. There is only *Self*, inside and outside of you, in everything that you see and experience, and *only* **when the human being re-seats the centre of consciousness from the head to the heart will things change for the better on your world.**

I would also like to talk about cycles today, because the heart beats to a cycle. There is a beat, then there is a gap; a beat and then a gap, and on Earth at the moment you are not living your lives in harmony with this natural cycle, which brings wellbeing to the individualisation of God that is the human being and also to all mankind. There has to be, just as there is a cycle in the day – you have day, then you have night – there has to be activity and rest, activity and rest; and your society has reached a time where there is no rest, *there is only activity.*

There is no daily withdrawal into the heart in order to contemplate God and to recharge the body with love; there is only activity on an outer, superficial level that degenerates and ages the body and corrupts the mind because the body and mind are constantly steeped in the illusion of your world and have no time to recover and heal. This is why you sleep.

Ancient civilisations knew that, in addition to sleep, contemplation was important and silence was paramount in examining the mysteries of life and in bringing forth the energies that are necessary for wellbeing whilst living within a physical shell.

You say now that life is being extended and that life expectancy is greater than it ever was, and that this is something new. This is not the case. It may surprise you to learn that the Ancients lived far longer within the human frame than you do now; *far longer...* and this was not a matter of diet, although diet had some part to play in it, but it was not solely diet. It was silence; it was contemplation; it was harmony; it was expansion from the heart-centre and living from the heart-centre. When one shifts one's consciousness from the head-centre to the heart-centre, the energies from the heart-centre irradiate the physical body and refine it and replenish it.

The energies from the head-centre, from the physical, complex thought-centre, are not able to do that. You cannot regenerate the physical body with logic, you have to regenerate it with love. You cannot heal people with logic, you have to regenerate people with love. And love comes not from the head-centre, which is analytical, but from the heart-centre, which is a mirror image of God.

It is no coincidence that so many souls are presently suffering with conditions that affect the heart-centre and the physical heart, because the heart-centre is under-nourished, it is under-considered, it is starved of the very energies that it is designed to give out; and your society is becoming reclusive. Oh, people seek out other people, and they exist in crowds, in cities and societies, but they are terribly insular because they are not used to touching each other via the heart-centre.

They are not used to exhibiting *true* love, which is not of the romantic kind, but is the spreading of God-Love via emanations through the heart-centre, through contemplation on and from that centre, and through moving the consciousness down from the head-centre to the heart-centre, so that all decisions that are made on behalf of other human beings and touch the lives of other souls are made with reference to what God-energy would do and how God-energy would treat the situation. In *all cases* God-energy would treat the situation with love, with creative force, not with the destruction we see in your world at this time.

There has to be a shift away from conventional religion towards spirituality and a more spiritual way of thinking, and not only in consciousness – there also has to be a shift in the way that those who are sitting for meditation are meditating. They have to learn to withdraw, not only from the outside world, but also from the clamour of the *inside* world that is created by the mechanisms and machinations of the head-centre.

Within each human being, within each soul, there is a chamber of peace; and that chamber of peace resides within the heart-centre. A meditation that many (as you would describe them) mystics, shamans, high priests and priestesses used to know and used to practise was one in which they would mentally go within that chamber, and lose themselves to the extent that all they felt, all they experienced during the meditation, was their pulse as a soul giving out into the physical and etheric universes. That is a lost art. They became – perhaps only for a second during their meditation – *pure Love*. In that instant they were transformed and they were then able to transform others through the energy stream that passed through them and emanated outwards from them. You have lost that ability as a species, and that is the sole reason why there is so much destruction at present.

The head says, 'I Want!' The heart says, 'I Give', and the mission we have from our 'vantage-point', if you like, from our reality, is to educate people into once again moving themselves into a state of consciousness where they can *give*. Souls cannot lose by giving, because the Heart of God is always pulsing out energy and, because the nature of God is cyclic, that energy eventually returns to the God-source, in part through the souls that are linking in with that God-source, bringing benefit and enlightenment to those souls.

So, nothing can ever be lost by giving; no one ever loses energy by giving out from the heart. By the fact that they absorb more God-energy by giving they become more God-like in thinking, because their thinking is not coming from the futile battleground that is the human physical mind.

Even in so-called spiritual religions today, those involved in such religions see a facet of the diamond of what they consider to be God-truth and become immersed in that, but they do not see the whole diamond. They do not realise that at the heart of that single facet they can see there is the Heart of God. This is what they should be striving for, to become one with the Heart of God through a change in consciousness.

I want to try and explain that energy emanates or radiates outwards from the point within the circle – from the Heart of God, if you like, at different frequencies at different times; and that each frequency that is sent out carries embedded within it a certain set of circumstances from which the various levels of reality are intended to benefit. So you might say that, depending on the nature of the pulse we are contained within, we are living in an age of the head, for example, or within an age of the heart, or in an age of upheaval, or in an age of growth, with the relevant circumstances and conditions that pertain to those various 'ages' coming about via the actions of the souls that are living within and responding to the radiations of those energies pulsating out from the Heart of God. The correct circumstances and conditions for growth are created because the souls within them are harmonising with the frequency of those vibrations.

It is a difficult concept to express in words. I am trying to explain that there are cycles to existence, there are pulses to existence, and that the souls living within those pulses can react to those radiations in different ways, but they are all tied up with certain intentions that emanate at specific lengths of 'time' (as you would understand it) from the Heart of God. And the pulse you exist within as souls at the moment is concerned with glorious spiritual growth but, unfortunately, it is not being tapped into in the right way.

You, therefore, see the *opposite* of the intention of the pulse manifesting around you. Everything has an opposite, otherwise it could not be; it only recognises itself by having an opposite that it can buffer against. Because the majority of souls are not harmonising with the radiation they are a part of, the radiation that is emanating around them at this time, they are experiencing its opposite. This is why there is so much cruelty and destruction and spiritual blindness at the moment.

You are actually living in the shadow. You have a phrase 'The Valley of the Shadow'. You are living in the shadow of what God's purpose really is for souls at this time. And the only way to come out of the dark side of this radiation is by shifting consciousness. That is the task of people who are spiritually motivated at this time; nothing more, nothing less... **simply to teach people to think from the heart and not from the head.**

We weep for the senseless destruction that is manifest on your world. Of course, the souls who are taken up in this destruction are ultimately not harmed, ultimately have played out a strategy, ultimately have been caught up only in a set of vibrations from which they have now been released but, nevertheless, on your physical level, that violence is potent. That violence is a radiation from the minds of men as opposed to the Heart of God. We are all God-like, we are all part of God, we have a choice in what we choose to create, and we weep for the chaos that exists on Earth at the moment *through choice.*

We weep – and then we get on with things, because we have to find openings through people who are willing to shake some sense into the rest of mankind, to show them a different way. And we note, not with amusement but certainly with a smile, that you are going through a book at the moment that contains the addresses of churches [*Michael: David and myself had at this time been looking through a book containing the addresses of certain spiritual centres with a view to writing to them to make them aware of a project we felt they would be interested in*]. Those churches are only tuning in to a facet and not to the heart of the diamond, yet they feel triumphant in a spiritual knowledge that really doesn't exist, for they have only scratched the surface and become enveloped and entranced by that surface vibration.

We pray for them, and we ask that you pray for them, and if anyone asks you what you do in your work spiritually, you are to say, 'It is my purpose to bring your soul to the heart of the matter.' And you will confuse them, but in their hearts they will know that you have touched upon a great spiritual truth.

The diamond shape as you recognise it on a pack of playing cards, but with a line through its centre so that you have four sides with a line through the centre, was our ancient representation of the heart. It has survived only in fruit machines and on playing cards, and without the line that used to bisect it. The line was there to signify the mirroring of God's Heart within the human heart.

So, once again, I have brought you a symbol. It is still a symbol of power because it was used for so long by so many civilisations. I am not for a moment suggesting that you have to use it, or any of the symbols I have brought to you, as symbols of power. I bring them through simply to acquaint you with them, and to acquaint you with the old ways, that in so many ways are better than the current ways. So it is the diamond shape with the line through the centre that was the original symbol of the heart, and not the heart symbol you now find in the pack of cards, which was invented long afterwards.

We invite you now to take your rest. We thank you for listening to us – there are many of us here today. I am your usual speaker, but there are also many others gathered, and we wish that we could talk in public places in the way we have spoken to you today, because we have noted the disruption in your capital [*Michael: a reference again to the London bombings.*]; we have noted the sadness and the grief. At times like this we long to make people see, but society turns a blind eye, and so we continue diligently to pray, and to take opportunities such as this to impart a little knowledge.

There are many of us standing here today, and we are sad that so little is understood after so long; and yet the Earth itself understands what we have said without speaking a word. The very rocks you stand on, that form the foundation of the world on which you walk and move and have your being, understand all of what we have said without us having to say it, yet the souls on Earth that are within physical shells do not.

If you would pray for people to great effect, then please use the symbol we have given you of the heart. It is a symbol of power – not in the foolish ways that people seek occult power on Earth – but because it is ancient, because it links to us. If you use it in meditation, see it in front of your forehead and see it beating out energy into the world, and you will make a difference during those times when you use it.

God bless and farewell for now.

Chapter Eight
Medicine

Michael's observations: You will perhaps find this to be Joseph's most shocking communication session to date. In it he has something very special and controversial to say to us regarding illness, its treatment, and our approach to health. He turns society's thinking on these subjects on its head, and we make no apologies for including the transcript in this book as we feel that Joseph is imparting vitally important information here, knowledge capable of transforming our lives and our states of wellbeing for the better and for life. If you find Joseph's observations on illness and medicine and accidents a bitter pill to swallow (forgive the pun) then we would respectfully suggest that you revisit this chapter at intervals to re-read it. David was, at first, a little shocked, though intrigued, by the words below. He has, however, listened to the recording we made of the session many times, and, over the months, has come to the conclusion that Joseph is absolutely right in his observations and that the key to perfect health lies within each of us as individuals.

What are my views on the contents of this session? Well, I was lucky enough to have sat in development for mediumship for many years with that remarkable spiritual teacher and old soul, Joan, who is mentioned at length in the introduction to this book. Her views on illness, presented to me some two decades ago, are very similar to Joseph's. During her long life she had proven to herself, in the face of seemingly overwhelming circumstances, time and time and time again, that mankind's approach to illness and disease is, for the most part, flawed, and, following an initial deep scepticism that gradually gave way to inner illumination as I tried out her theories and proved them for myself, so have I.

Here's Joseph on Medicine…

Joseph: I wish today to talk about medicine and to start with one of my statements, which will set the cat amongst the pigeons:

There is nothing wrong with you.

This is a message for all of mankind – *There is nothing wrong with you.*

Because you are a vibration, because you are a soul, you are perfection and you are a part of God. And, as nothing is wrong with God – God is an ongoing state of perfection, a cyclic state of perfection – you are a mirror of that perfection. From cradle to grave, in your terms, you are perfect.

How, then, can it be that there is so much illness, so much malady in the world? This stems from a misconception of what you are. It stems from treating a 'coating', from applying healing energy to a place where healing energy cannot go. You can only alter the centre, you cannot alter the surround, the shell, the physical body. In your society, and in current thinking around the world, the shell is approached and seemingly healed and altered. Then you say, 'We have brought back health, we have altered the state of the being and brought back health.' But you cannot do that. No doctor can do that. No shaman can do that. No one can do that because *health is yours automatically*. You cannot alter the perfection of God that flows through you! What you have to alter is attitude. What true medicine should be on your level is an altering of attitude, because it is the human attitude that is wrong, that creates the illusion of illness. Illness is separation. Illness is resistance. Illness is unhappiness. Illness is a tendency to surround oneself with the baser vibrations rather than to look upwards and inwards at the perfection that is mankind's as souls.

The true doctor, or the doctors that will come to your world eventually as souls incarnated in matter, will be people who can help souls to get in touch with themselves again, who can guide them back towards the centre, who can penetrate this shell of illusion and say, 'This is who you are... this is why you are here... this is what you are capable of.' True medicine – healing – can be likened to the stripping away of the shells of vibrations that souls have placed around themselves and believe to be their true state. They dream illness... I'll repeat that... **they *dream* illness**. Illness is conjured up... and it is *attractive*.

Illness attracts sympathy, for example. It also attracts to itself illnesses from other souls; other, similar vibrations from other souls. It is a mini-illusion within your societal illusion, if you like, within the greater illusion that is the Earth plane. And this is what you, as souls, do; you create, within the greater illusion, lesser illusions that you place around yourselves and believe to be true, and illness is one of those illusions. Medicine is also an illusion because it is the transference of power from God into a pill ...or a scalpel ...or a doctor ...or a surgeon ...or a nurse. It is a transference of faith in God into any of those people or things.

And that is why, very often, the patient appears to get better, because they are so full of faith in the pill, or the potion, or the lotion, or the bonesetter, or the man with the scalpel, that they elevate them to the state of the God-within ...and they cure themselves. But really the pill has done nothing; the surgeon has done nothing; the nurse has done nothing. It is the patient that has projected faith from inside themselves outwards onto that person or potion, has believed in that person or potion as a means to their wellness – their wholeness – again, and therefore they have made themselves well.

So it is with many people. This is why you can have two people with exactly the same symptoms, treated by the same surgeon, and one will recover and one will not; because the wish of the one is to recover, and the wish of the other is to die.

Isn't that sad? It is the wish of the other to leave this world...

Yes, we know that karmic influences must also be considered in such a case, but that wish to die can also come from a past life and can be something that a soul repeats, can bring into this illusion with them from a past life – the desire to die; the desire to leave here; the desire to be steeped in sorrow. They then leave the world abruptly, as though they are saying to the universe, 'I told you so!' And on and on they go. They incarnate again, and go through it again, until they realise that God is within them, that they can never die, they can never be ill, and they then let go of the pattern they have placed around themselves.

The way in which you treat people medically on Earth at the moment is very basic, is very unenlightened. And it will take an age before people are treated in the right way, because there is a demand from people that they be treated in a certain way. They expect the scalpel, they expect the pill, they expect to be separated from friends and family, to be in hospital... they expect to go through pain and discomfort; that is the only way they know of to cure themselves. And when they have gone through this process, they then decide whether they are going to be healthy or whether they are going to move on, to die.

Therefore, you have set up a society in which there are people who can supply that demand. There is the doctor who will separate you from your friends and family when you are 'ill', and this should never be done because it is love that changes the pattern within people and penetrates the shells that people place around themselves. There are doctors and nurses who will put you through discomfort, who will put you through pain, who will put you through an agony of wondering whether you are going to recover or not, because that is what you expect of them, that is your medicine. And so you make yourself ill, and then you decide whether you will cure yourself or not; and you decide on the degree of pain you will put yourself through in the meantime.

So, there is never a vengeful God decreeing that you must be ill, there is only cause and effect; but that cause and effect does not apply to the core – to the soul. That soul is perfect, that soul knows nothing of illness because that soul comes from and exists within a realm where there is no illness, there is no decay, there is no lack, there is nothing only the God that that soul is a part of ...and that God is perfect.

So, the illness is a projection around that soul, and no matter what the soul appears to go through whilst it is on Earth (and we've touched on this before in earlier conversations) it is not really going through those circumstances.

The medicine that is needed at the moment is *education*. People need to know who they are, but they do not accept who they are. It is easier to go along with the illusion.

I must also touch on the point that many people want to be ill... *they want to be ill*. It is a focus for attention. It is a way not to involve yourselves in the things that seem to be so difficult for you on Earth. You do not have to work, you do not have to be nice to people; because when you're ill all is forgiven. 'They're ill!' and all is, therefore, excusable.

People need that perspective of the soul. To understand that they are souls, to understand that what they go through in life is only a suit of clothes, or several suits of clothes, of which illness is just one. To understand that when their attitude – their perspective – is changed, then the illness disappears, because, in the mind, at some point in its spiritual evolution, a light goes on, and the person says, 'I'm not ill. How can I be ill? I am more than this; I am not this at all. This is simply something that I am putting myself through.' And so medicine at the moment is simply a complex placebo. No matter whether they are operating on the brain or the big toe, or giving out pills or prescriptions, it is a placebo. The whole thing is a placebo.

The medical profession does not understand what it does, and the souls who think they are ill do not understand illness! How can things change? Things *will* change. I foresee for you at some stage in your future centres in which people will sit to raise their vibrations, not to communicate in the way that we are doing today, but to raise their vibrations; to lift themselves up and out of the illusion for a time, to make the illusion their tool and not their master. And to link up to the great chain of souls that exists around this globe, and to eventually link up to the chain of souls that exits on other planes and in other spheres.

In simply sitting, and in remembering who they are, and in reaching out to each other in love, they will heal themselves. They will lift themselves above illness, and they will dose out medicine to the world.

This is the next step for churches or people who wish to sit for the Light. Not to sit in constant conversation with us. We are not here to chat; we are here to change things. And we look forward to the day when people will sit to bring Light to themselves and to others – the *true* medicine – to raise everyone above the illusion so that, when they are dropped back into it, they will see it as an illusion, and see it as a tool to be used to further the evolution of their soul.

There will be a time when souls leave this level of consciousness as easily as walking through an open door. They will not be ill, they will simply realise and feel the pull that tells them they are changing, that they have come to the end of one circle of circumstance and are entering another one. They will not die ill, and transition will not be feared. This is part of God's plan, that transition should not be feared, for it is only a matter of going through a 'door' into another 'room'.

Disease is belief; epidemic is belief. Epidemics... disease... these are not transmitted by microbes; they are not transmitted by germs. They are transmitted by belief: belief at the individual soul level and belief at a group soul level on Earth. And that, again, is why some will contract flu and some will not. It is the measure of belief in the disease that brings it to you, and nothing to do with the micro-organisms that are always blamed for disease.

Illness, as you are aware, is a reflection of what is wrong – what is perceived to be wrong – and what is *ill at ease* within the soul, and illness attacks the body in an area that corresponds to what is wrong with a soul spiritually.

The heart is heavy... the head is confused... the back will not support... the knees go... (and, yes, we do apply that to you). [*Michael: in that last comment Joseph is talking directly to me and referring to a problem I had or, rather, I was accepting that I had, at the time*]. The ego is bruised... the ribs are bruised... the heart is bruised... yet none of these things can be possible. **Illness is a diagnosis of what is wrong with the soul.**

We have to also include in this session a comment on accident, because accident also occurs by the soul's volition. You will say that no one wants to be in an accident, but an accident can also bring to attention what a soul perceives as being wrong in its situation, with its existence on Earth.

There are no such things as accidents. From a tumble to a car-crash, it is not an accident, it is by design. It is the will of the souls involved in the 'accident' to work out certain vibrations around them, vibrations that link them together through the accident for the purposes of doing so.

So, disease does not exist and accidents do not exist. Everything is by design; by design of the soul... and what a different world you would have if you realised this! The way to cure oneself at this stage in your evolution is by letting go of the illness, by not acknowledging it, by letting it fall away and saying that it is not part of you. Say, 'I am separate from it', and it will fall away, because it has no purchase on the soul, it has no power. It is only the power given to it by the soul that allows it to exist.

This is why hypnosis can be effective... the hypnotist reaches inwards to the point of existence of the soul at which the two minds meet, and the hypnotist says, 'Wouldn't it be a good idea if you let go of this illness/worry/belief?' This is why hypnosis works, but again it can only work if the soul is willing to let that hypnosis work on itself/him/herself.

Self-hypnosis is possible. Souls can actually convince themselves that they are not ill, that no harm can come to them, by drawing on the power of the God-within, the creative power of God, but at present this power is always used – or almost always used – negatively on your plane.

It is a strange experience for us to walk through a hospital, because in a hospital we find people who are not ill. Yet the people there are putting themselves to death... but they cannot die! It is a madhouse from our point of view. We do not criticise it, and we do all we can to help to heal; but in healing, all we are doing is reinforcing the magnetic energies of the soul.

We cannot heal the body because the body is illusion. All we can heal is the soul's concept of the body. Once we have done that successfully then the body is healed because the illusion has been altered. We give strength to the soul's concept that the body is whole and cannot be ill.

Our other problem is that we do try and work with doctors and with healers and with counsellors, but all too often we come up against arrogance, the arrogance that says, 'I can heal.'

What can you heal? If there is nothing to heal, *what can you heal? What can you possibly heal?* We try to get into the minds of doctors and nurses and people who purport to heal others and to make them aware that they can only heal – as a concept – when they have reached into the soul they are attempting to heal; when they understand that soul. **In making that soul understand itself healing takes place.**

Healing is nothing more than a dropping away of the vibrations that that soul is being hindered by... is being held back by. Once that takes place, healing takes place, the soul is strengthened in its perception of itself as being perfect and it moves on... until it next believes that it is ill and needs medicine in some way.

There is a great swell of disease around the heart at the moment on your Earth... a hardening of hearts... literally, a hardening of hearts, which is again due to the number of souls that have chosen to divorce themselves mentally, in concept, from God. They can never, of course, be divorced from God, but they have chosen to be so. To resist loving; to resist giving; and that resistance creates a hardness in the vibrations around the soul which relate to the heart chakra. As a result of this you will see an increase of heart disease in years to come to alarming proportions. It is nothing to do with food; it is nothing to do with lifestyle... it is to do with thought, as all things are. It is to do with the individualisation that has been taken to the n'th degree on this planet and must be relinquished.

Souls have a need for each other. They have to come back to a time when there is co-operation and an inter-dependence between all souls, but at this present point in time souls seem to have distanced themselves so far from God, and it is resulting in illness. It is resulting in a need for medicine. We would ask that you pray for souls on a daily basis, and radiate the White Light around the globe. See it touching the hearts, particularly of the souls that are here now, but also of the younger generation, because they have taken onboard 'the Sins of the Fathers'. By this I mean that if you incarnate to certain parents, then you inherit not just their physical characteristics, but you pass through their karmic cycles and you take on some of that karma yourself. And part of that karma, at the moment, is the hardening of the heart.

So, the younger generation needs to be prayed for, because many of them have extraordinary spiritual abilities, but those abilities can only come to the fore via their evolution. So the White Light is needed – that is the medicine I recommend at this time for mankind.

You will also see (which seems to be going from one extreme to the other) an increased incidence of problems with the skin... with rashes and eruptions of the skin. This concerns certain souls who are on Earth, who have completed various cycles and keep coming back to Earth, not being happy with themselves. They want to be someone else. They want to be out of the skin they are in... and you will think that their irritation is down to allergies. There is new information – news – coming presently of something that is attacking the skin. Some will perceive this as a new skin disease... and you will see this in your papers and your magazines, but it is in reality a manifestation of a soul-wish to be someone else; always to be someone else, never to be happy with who you are.

So, watch for the heart and watch for the skin, because these two areas in mankind are affected greatly at this time by illness. But the medicine – the *cure* – needs to come from within, and from people like yourselves who will, please God, pray for others.

I have spoken enough.

Now that we have touched upon this subject, maybe you will be able to recognise trends within people; to recognise the discontent in them today that will lead to illness for them tomorrow.

God bless you both.

Michael: (to David) He's gone...

Chapter Nine
Nothing

Michael's observations: During the early days of sitting for communication with Joseph, before Jane joined us, David and myself found that, at times, due to work constraints or personal pressures, our 'regular', monthly, afternoon appointment to bring through information from him would sometimes have to be cancelled. We always felt bad about this, little realising that Joseph has a very different sense of time than we do, as his reassurances to us in this chapter reveal.

During this session he talks at length about 'Nothing' and, I'm certain, as Joseph has quite a sense of humour, that he finds that last statement amusing.

Also apparent during this communication is the extent to which Joseph had begun to control my mind and speech by 'overshadowing' me whenever he spoke through me. Increasingly I felt as though I was simply a bystander – an observer listening to and watching myself being used by Joseph (completely willingly, of course). If I was unsure about something he was saying, or my personality questioned it because it was a new concept I hadn't considered before, (such as Joseph's reference to God and 'Nothing' within the text) then, because I was allowing him to use my mind and vocal chords to an increasing extent whilst we were linked, I found myself hard placed to override his words and interject my own. I was, of course, free to comment and express my opinions following a communication, but it was essential that I did not break the link by bringing my own personality into play during the precious time in which Joseph is allowed to speak through me.

Joseph: Today I want to talk about *Nothing*. I have been trying to inspire Michael with thoughts on this subject for some eight weeks and I have managed to get through in his less fraught moments [*Michael: I was going through a 'challenging' period at this time, during which my experience of each day could be graded into 'very fraught', 'less fraught' or, in exceptional circumstances, simply 'fraught'!*]

'Nothing' is a fascinating subject and something that the soul works towards subconsciously, because, in rejecting everything corporeal and material, the soul gains insight into everything yet realises, at the same time, *that there is no everything – that there is nothing there.*

I should talk about simplicity as well, because the two go hand in hand – nothing and simplicity. **The way forward for souls is through nothing and simplicity.** This is one of the great problems you encounter in your age, in that for many souls on Earth nothing is nothing, and nothing is simple. You attach, as conscious beings, weight and significance to every object that you come across; to every concept you come across; and you attach degrees of significance, of importance, to objects and to occurrences. You draw everything out of the Nothing, but instead of returning concepts to the Nothing when you have finished with them, you are solidifying those concepts constantly and they then become a barrier around you – like bricks, like a turret in a castle that surrounds a prisoner.

This creates a difficulty we find when many souls return to the ...if you like ... 'nothingness' from which they came. I do not mean non-existence, I mean nothingness materially, corporeally, because they have attached such great significance to objects, to concepts, to ideas, to beliefs whilst on Earth that these things often have to be chipped away at from within the soul in order for it to realise that it has moved on.

Let me give you an example to illustrate what I mean. If I think of a chair on my level of understanding – from my place of being – then that chair appears, but it is only a tool for my soul. If I am presenting myself in a corporeal form, then I might wish to sit on a chair, so I materialise a chair from the void – from proto-matter, if you like. I materialise a chair, I sit on it, and, when I no longer have a use for it, I simply draw my attention away from it and the chair returns to the proto-matter from which it came, as though it had never been. The proto-matter is infinite; it can create anything that I wish it to create within the confines of my experience. But once I have de-materialised that chair by putting my attention out elsewhere, I don't need it any more. I don't strap it to me and carry it around with me because I might sometime have need for a chair ...**but the souls on Earth do just that with every object they assign value to.** It can be a chair, or a cup, or an ideal; it can be a belief or a prejudice; it can be an emotion; it can be a pain or a loss. All of these things are not of the soul, they are simply aspects of 'reality' on the Earth-level of consciousness that people perceive at certain times, then decide to carry along with them indefinitely.

This is why the human body, the human structure – which also comes from nothing – ages faster than it should do. At your point in evolution you should be living longer than you do, but your quality of living has actually diminished. You may have machines that keep the body alive, but you have very little that keeps the soul alive. You have created for yourselves a living hell because you drag along with you, like Marley's Ghost, the baggage of life on so many different levels.

Even in meditation souls make it so difficult for their minds to be free of the concepts around them. What a fabulous meditation for people to stop daily and say: 'I exist. All exists. Nothing exists.' Try it: **'I exist. All exists. Nothing exists.'** What a fabulous meditation, because it takes away – in contemplation of those words – the walls you put around yourselves that restrict you spiritually.

You see, the human mind – the evolutionary mind – is programmed *against* Nothing. It feels there has to be *something*. The reasoning mind wants *something* – there has to be *something* tomorrow; there has to be *something* after death. But the something that the mind perceives, that the mind wants, is not the something that awaits. That something is existence and existence is nothing to do with Nothing.

Nothing is a state of rest of the field through which all material things are drawn. 'Ether', if you like. Proto-matter, as I have said. It is an infinite, creative tool.

You, David, have drawn in the past. You, Michael, make your models. [*Michael: Joseph knows us well. David has an artistic background, I have made models for as long as I can remember. Our hobbies are what he is referring to here.*] In doing these things you are both drawing from the pool, and you are solidifying through creativity what you desire to witness in front of you at a particular time. This is what we, as souls, also do, but we don't do it with an easel or with tools, we do it by thinking, by using the palette of the mind, the palette of the spirit, to create what we want from the ether around us.

This does not mean for a moment that we exist in a void; but we are aware of the void existing... if something that is Nothing can exist, that is. You see the paradox? I am trying to put this into earthly terms and into earthly words. It doesn't mean that we exist in a white limbo or in a mist. We exist in a state we find comfortable, and that is our right as souls who are evolving, and we have to have points of sensory reference.

For example, if I wanted to visit you and to talk to you and you and I were both on my level of existence, then we would 'draw' around us familiar surroundings, surroundings we were both comfortable with – somebody's house or a park, for example – and then, when we had finished, all of these things would go away and be stored in the proto-matter or in the 'ether', as it were, until we needed them again. What I am trying to say is that, with each step we put in front of our feet (and feet is a relative term here) what we need at that particular time, but we're not locked into that landscape to the extent that it blinds us; that it cripples us; that it imprisons us, and this is what is wrong with the Earth plane at the moment.

This is why communication from the spirit side is still such a difficult thing, and it shouldn't be. At this point in your evolution, communication with other fields – other vibrations – should be quite simple.

The human race has steeped itself in its constructs and has complete faith in those constructs – which are perceived as being outside of itself – and no faith at all from within; in the God-within. At this point in your evolution you should be drawing more from the God-within and less from the constructs 'outside' of you, and you would then hear and see us quite easily, and we would then give demonstrations – using a medium, yes – but we would be able to materialise, as you would understand it, and talk to congregations, talk to all those who would be willing to listen; but this barrier of heavy constructs prevents communication taking place as it should do at this time.

The natural state of the universe is Nothing. This doesn't mean there is nothing there. I am trying to show Michael (he is trying to struggle against my words and to put his opinion in, but I'm not letting him) that God and Nothing... yes... *they are the same thing*. But the intelligence is not part of the Nothing; the Nothing is the tool. The Nothing, as I have said, is the palette, the easel, the sculptor's clay, and we, as individualisations of God, are the sculptors.

The road has been made too complex. The road for many who profess to understand spiritual things has been made too complex, because they will not allow themselves time to indulge in Nothing. If a part of each day was used to meditate, to understand that your 'reality' is a field that can go back to Nothing *according to your will* then, as you mentally took back to Nothing the things around you that you did not need, you would release yourself from illnesses. You would release yourself from vibrations you may have picked up from other people, that have been clinging to them because they acknowledge them as having power, and are now clinging to you because so do you, subconsciously.

You should consider regularly reverting all to Nothing by simply saying, 'I am' – and this is what Jesus talked about, this is what *I am* means – it means *I am* and nothing else is necessary, and that is all you need to know. If you were to contemplate that for a short time each day you would become healthier, you would become more focused on the things that do matter in life, and all problems in life would be solved from *within*. You would make redundant your lawyers and your doctors and your counsellors, because they deal with problems of the material. You may argue that counsellors don't deal with the material, they deal with problems of the mind. They are dealing with *solidified beliefs*; that is what they are trying to shift, that is what they are trying to move. Solidified beliefs. People say, 'I am ill.' 'I have got this problem.' 'There is this injury that occurred to me when I was a child and I can't let it go.' You can't let it go because you *won't* let it go. You won't let it go back to Nothing.

The Buddhists are mistaken. They strive for Nothing, yes, but they strive for obliteration of the consciousness, which cannot happen. There is only consciousness and the Field, and the consciousness and the Field are one, but the consciousness is not the Nothing. I know that sounds like a paradox. The consciousness is the consciousness. The Field is created and activated by the consciousness as a tool, but it is not the consciousness. The consciousness runs through the Field to enable it to form into the myriad shapes and ideas that are possible within the Field, but the Field is not conscious in the way that the consciousness is conscious. Don't break the communication! [*Michael: I became a little confused by Joseph's meaning at this point, but Joseph insisted, quite rightly, that I maintain the link*]. The consciousness is the controller of the Field and also the creator of the Field. The Field is the child of the consciousness but it is not the consciousness, and this is the mistake people make. They imbue the Field with its own volition. Its volition, its trends, its manifestations come from the wills of the consciousness – from the desires of the souls who manipulate it.

There has to come a time when the people on Earth abandon and let go of their grip on material possessions, but again they get this wrong. They say, 'In order to find enlightenment I must forego all material possessions!' No! If you were instead to forego them *for a few moments each day*, you would get them into perspective and then you could bring them back out of the Field, enjoy them and put them away again for the next day, with clarity as to what to do each day of your lives. But no, again there is this misapprehension that all material things must disappear in order to find enlightenment. Not so! You are living in a particular density – a particular vibration – of the universal field and material things brought out of the field are your tools, not your masters. That is the distinction I am making.

It is as much of an error to say, 'I must forego all material things' as to say, 'I embrace all material things and nothing else.' They are tools. They are Nothing.

You have speculated over the several weeks since we last spoke as to whether our communication had been required earlier; as to whether I needed to speak to you on a regular basis according to your timescale. Again, that is a belief. I have not been criticising you because we are meeting at a later point than usual. It is only a belief that there has been a break of months between us having spoken last and us speaking today. *There has been no break.*

All that has happened is that you have perceived different aspects of the Field. I would say 'for a time', but to say 'for a time' is wrong as well, because no time has passed. You have perceived a set of circumstances, a set of values of the Field, and now here we are, speaking together again, but there has been no break. This is why I can speak so easily after, from your point of view, months of not being here.

And I know that you have speculated at times as to where I live. I live, like you, within a field; and I am showing Michael at the moment a view of what he perceives to be a green crystal, which seems to spread around his vision, but this is just an image of somewhere I am at the moment. I am using the energy from that crystal to communicate with you. I do live somewhere, but I take my abode, if you like, with me as a (in computer terms) 'downloadable' environment. So that if I wish to communicate with other people within my expression of the field, my range of vibrations, I simply call upon them from the Nothing, and then we are together, and we can put around us whichever environment we choose to so that we can communicate, and then those environments are collapsed back into the Nothing.

There is a great pleasure in spending a great deal of time immersed in the Nothing, because in the Nothing all kinds of concepts and communications and constructs and blossomings of thought are possible. Indeed, we do sit as a number of souls – a number of expressions of God – to indulge in what you would perhaps describe as 'think-tanks'; to experience the wonder of Creation, the wonder of the *I am*, and we draw great pleasure from being close to other expressions of God, to other souls. There is great pleasure in communication. There is great pleasure in simply being with another expression of God.

This is something mankind has also lost. By placing, as a race, such value on material things you miss the opportunity simply to be with another soul... to be, *to be*... without communication; just to – in love – experience the one-ship of all souls.

What a fabulous gift! And what a fabulous gift you are missing on Earth! What a fabulous gift you are not experiencing, because so many of your relationships are tied up with solidifications from the Field, so you cannot have a relationship without the relationship being tied into a car, a house, a fridge, some food, some clothes, some money.

You cannot just have a relationship. Tied into the mental field of the souls within a relationship are material expectations, when the only expectation should be, 'I love to be with you... and together let us experience more of being.' That is a relationship. That is love – not the twisted expectations of many couples on Earth at this time.

These are not love of one another. These are love, if you think about it, of constructs from the Field. It is not love of the soul, it is love of the construct of the Field that you see before you – the physical appearance – and think that you love, but it is also love of the constructs in the energy field of the soul that you are linking to.

When at its purest, love is simply, 'I love you and wish to be'... not 'with you' as you understand it, because that is confining, but 'with you' in the sense of being one with you, at peace with you, in harmony with you, at one with your wishes and desires, at one with the direction your vibration – our vibration – is taking you/us in. I love you and wish to *be* with you... and if you wish to *be* with me, to *be*-come with me, to co-create an existence with me, we will experience things together from this point onwards.

So, love is a shedding of things, of material things, and comes back to this concept of the Field being a tool. True love does not come with conditions – with concepts from the Field – attached to it. It doesn't come with baggage, yet it is tending to do so at this moment on Earth.

Relationships on Earth are suffering because they are often not true relationships. You invest time and value in the transitory perception of what someone looks like, but built into that surface concept of the person you love is a natural decay that is part of the Field, generated by aeons of the Field operating in the way it does at present. The vehicle, the façade, has to decay and change, but people love the façade and not the soul. Once they learn to love the soul things will change, relationships will be perceived as permanent because they are known to be so from the soul, and will not be based on a physical attraction that fades so rapidly.

I have tired the instrument. I wished to talk about Nothing, and in doing so to perhaps give you some encouragement and enlightenment, to tell you that you are on the right path, are in the right way of thinking [*Michael: here Joseph is talking to, encouraging, David and myself*]. You have surmised as much over the years, realising that nothing that 'is', even though it can give you pleasure, is permanent. However, souls arrive here all the time having left your band of vibration and they are desperately tugging with them vibrations that should be left behind.

There is, of course, the saying 'you can take nothing with you' ...you take nothing with you. *Of course you do*, because Nothing is all there is around you, yet that Nothing is full of the somethings you have chosen to create within it, and many souls try to pull with them into the greater worlds the constructs they have invested so much time and energy into whilst on Earth, which restrict them until they learn to think in another way and until they learn to let go.

In leaving I say to you, 'Nothing matters', and I would like you to think of those two words: **Nothing matters...**

There is a deep secret, a deep truth, within the phrase *Nothing matters* because Nothing *does* matter. It matters that you realise that your perception of everything is malleable dependent on your wishes, because that is how you will operate when you come to the higher side of life, and that is how you operate now if you were only to acknowledge it. I am preaching to souls that know this already [*Michael: myself and David.*] but it does no harm to re-awaken those energies within you.

Nothing matters.

What you bring out of and release back into the Nothing matters.

In times when you cannot get around things, around your situations on Earth, remember that *Nothing matters* and you will see the nonsense of the situations around you and they will melt away. In your times of greatest stress ...Nothing matters. The material that is in front of you does not matter. No thing in the Field matters. Knowing that you can take things back to the Nothing in an instant by concentrating on them then letting them go will release you from many of the trials that you undergo on a physical level.

And we will talk again in June...

Michael: Gone.

Chapter Ten
The Heart Seed

Michael's observations: With this session the duo that had sat for so long became a trio, as David and myself were joined for the first time for a Joseph communication by my beloved Jane, who would, from this point onwards, add her energy, enthusiasm and unique viewpoints to our proceedings. We now sat mostly in the evenings, and around David's dining table at his new house rather than in our old attic venue. As a parallel expansion of our capabilities, and due to Jane and myself becoming a couple, Jane's employer, Peter, brought his own unique contribution to the project. Jane lent Peter the Joseph recordings we had made to date, and, having been a seeker of spiritual truth for some time, (nothing is coincidence – we meet the people we are supposed to meet) he was instantly impressed by them – so much so that he told us he wanted to transcribe each and every recording, which was music to the ears of David and myself. Due to pressures of work and personal demands on our time neither of us had been able to even attempt a start on this massive undertaking, and Peter's diligence in turning the Joseph recordings into the written word moved us considerably closer to the day when this book could be published.

Joseph: The subject of tonight's lecture is the 'Seed'. The Seed of Heart Consciousness is the topic I wish to talk about, and I will open by telling you that the consciousness of the individual *changes* as the owner of that consciousness progresses as a soul.

Spiritual consciousness begins as a 'seed', if you like, and it is the heart consciousness I am referring to here and not the consciousness of the head-mind or the consciousness of the physical body. The heart consciousness is the recorder of everything that happens to and everything that is experienced by a soul, and the heart consciousness is brought into operation by 'external' forces whilst a soul is on Earth, by situations that are purposely sent to the soul to help that soul to dislodge its thinking from the head consciousness.

Sometimes lifetimes can be spent by a soul during which it will operate from the head consciousness only; lifetimes in which the ability to record and assimilate data is the only preoccupation of the occupant of a physical body; lifetimes in which the heart consciousness is totally masked and muted, with all decisions being made from the point of view of the head, from what is between the ears. Then, gradually, over lifetimes, over long periods of time, certain lessons are set up for the soul, which stimulate the heart. Not the physical heart, you understand, but the seed of consciousness that is actually buried – located – at this point within the physical body.

If you were able to see my spiritual appearance at this moment you would perceive me as a sphere. We have talked about the sphere – the circle – previously, as being the nature of

God and the nature of existence, and this spherical nature is reflected in the chakras, in the spiritual energy centres. Here at my heart-centre [*Michael: Joseph is using my hand to tap my heart-centre at this point.*] and encompassing my solar plexus, I manifest a large sphere of light, which I have accumulated, which I have refined, over many existences and countless experiences.

I am speaking to you now through here [*Michael: again, an indication of the heart chakra.*] because here is *what I am*, and if you were able to see us on higher spheres of existence you would see us as spheres; you would not see us as human at all, because the more our consciousness is raised, the more we appear as spheres of Light on a certain vibration. As I have said to you before, we can also manifest as formless consciousness on other vibrations of being, because we are simply an expression of energy, and, on others still, we can appear as you do, as completely human, if we so wish.

With many people, were you to look at them with spiritual, with psychic eyes, you would see that there is only the beginning of a sphere at this point, at the heart-centre. It would look like a flat disk. It needs to be nurtured like any seed, and it is nurtured by steps of emotional progression; sets of lessons; sets of promptings that are brought to the soul to begin the expansion of the seed within the heart.

We talked some time ago about the dot within the circle, the symbol of God. At the heart-centre there is the seed, the dot within the circle that begins to grow through the emotional pressures and tides that are placed around each soul. Were you able to see my brethren, my contemporaries, and were you able to see some of the souls from 'above' my level of existence, you would notice this great blossoming of colour and of power from

121

their hearts, spreading from the heart and the solar plexus outwards, from the seat of spiritual existence and consciousness. This expansion of spirituality is what we are trying to stimulate in human beings on Earth at this time, or, rather, I should say the Great Spirit, God, is working to stimulate this growth.

You may think your life is unique, that the trials you are going through and have endured no one else has ever gone through, that the challenges you face no one else has ever faced, and that your unique circumstances can never be repeated with any other soul. You are not as unique as you believe yourself to be, because similar sets of emotional challenges are brought to each spirit in different guises so that the heart-centre can begin to vibrate at a higher frequency. There is no situation you have gone through that another soul has not gone through before. True, you may have different points of reference within those situations, you may approach them uniquely, but the underlying situation is essentially the same as it has been for so many other souls because it is brought into play by God. Each soul, including you, has to go through very similar circumstances of learning in order for its heart-centre to be opened.

Now I want you to consider this next point very carefully. You probably believe that each person's karma is different. Yes, it is, if you compare it at any one time, if you take 'snapshot photographs', as it were, and compare one person's karma at a frozen point in time with another person's karma frozen at that same point in time. However, the experiences of both souls viewed from the point of view of the totality of what those souls are learning from their karma are very similar, are **essentially the same experience**, because each soul has to learn from the same lessons.

Each soul has to have its heart seed stimulated and, as that heart seed becomes stimulated, as the vibration within the heart is stimulated, then the soul's consciousness begins to change, because the outpouring of refined energy from this centre begins to affect the other centres within the body, and begins to irradiate the lower mind, the physical mind, with a higher vibration. Then the mind begins to change, and the purpose in expanding the heart-centre is to bring the physical mind eventually under the control of the true seat of spiritual consciousness, the heart-mind.

One of the problems with existence on Earth at the moment is that people are stimulated by data and not by the heart. There is a great spiritual movement presently from our side that involves the use of the silver vibration and the attentions of a number of souls who are, as you might describe them, Masters of Karma. On a certain frequency – a certain vibration – there is a stimulation on the Earth plane via the silver vibration to bring people to their knees so that they will begin to think with their hearts and not with their minds. Much of what you see happening around you; much of the destruction that you witness at the moment, is as a result of that process, because we have to try and filter out of individuals this reliance on things being, as they currently judge them through the physical mind, so black and white in the physical world. The violence you are witnessing now is as a result of the struggle to re-seat consciousness in individuals from the mind to the heart.

I know it doesn't seem that way to you. It looks like there is war, destruction, inhumanity... but the souls involved in these circumstances are struggling. The souls who perpetrate the violence are struggling. They are trying to come to terms with their perception of their world being different than they think it is, with the re-location of their consciousness.

Only when the individual consciousness has been relocated to the heart can it grow.

Only when the individual consciousness has been relocated to the heart-centre can man truly experience the spirit worlds, because they are not worlds of logic, they are not worlds of matter as yours is. They are worlds that have to be appreciated through love, and how can you appreciate anything centred in love when you are centred in logic?

Around the year 2020 you will find there is a shift. There will be a shift in consciousness then, in thinking; from thinking from a matter-based thought to a perception of the finer values. We promise you it is not that far away. From Australia there will come a truly remarkable display of spiritual understanding from someone who is already on Earth but has not yet shown this tendency.

Anything that is worth having has to be born in struggle, and it is struggle you are witnessing at this time. You are moving into a period we would call a 'fluid time'. We would describe it as a time of water and of water signs. During this time there will be great change, and the beginning of the change, a change of vibration, will come around 2016. It will appear until that time as though things are being taken to the brink, and *they are*. Conditions have to be tested. They have to be pushed to the point where people say, 'Enough of this... there must be another way!' Only by letting souls take themselves to the brink can you help them to discover, to *rediscover* their true identity, their true selves. So, there is a slow shift in thinking from the head to the heart, which is happening at this time.

Once people acknowledge that they come from here [*Michael: again, Joseph indicates my heart-centre.*] your world will change. The world came close to doing this a long time ago... a *long* time ago... but it wasn't ready for the change in thinking. People lost sight of the spiritual goal. They lost sight of their motivation. The potential for change was lost. This time it *will* work, and you will all live long enough to see great change, wondrous change, and you will say, 'Well, finally, something is happening! Finally something is happening.'

I am delighted to be able to talk to you again this evening after what has seemed like a large gap between communications for all of you, and I welcome the lady into the group. Jane, you have been known about for quite some time, and I thank you for the benefits you bring to any meeting, and to Michael at this moment, by lending your vibrations, by giving your vibrations to him so that he can work on a more refined level of consciousness. And I must say to you that the vibrations that you give to him come from the heart – where else would they come from?

It might interest you to know that the smoke you are burning [*Michael: David had been burning incense to cleanse the room prior to our meeting.*] has colour, and I am able to see that colour because I am on a higher level of consciousness than you are at this time. As the soul's consciousness expands more of God's glories are visible, and you are operating on a very low frequency of vibration in the spectrum with regard to what you are presently able to see and appreciate.

Again I must return to why there are problems in your world. It is because the instigators of those problems are operating on that low wavelength, that low spectrum of what they are able to see. Once they begin to perceive with the heart-mind things will begin to expand as they see and sense more spiritually.

To sum up: heart consciousness is a seed, a true God-part of the human, sentient being which seeks to grow, but it is masked by the physical mind acting as a computer, as a switchboard, as a censor to truth, and by the physical mind believing that what it sees is the only level of existence possible.

Gradually the heart seed has to open, the God-child within the physical framework has to manifest itself and work its way through the denser vibrations of the physical body and the physical mind in order to evolve.

When you pray, always pray for the growth of the God-seed within in all souls on Earth. Always consider that precious energy that one day will manifest itself on this and on other levels of consciousness as pure Light, pure consciousness and pure love.

Chapter Eleven
The Female Principle

Michael: Joseph is telling me he would like to talk about the feminine aspect of creation tonight. He says that the topic will be a two-parter, and that it is the feminine side he wishes to cover on this occasion.

He is talking about the moon, and about the silver vibration, and about the water vibration; and he says there is a need for expansion of the feminine side on Earth at the moment. There is a need to produce more of the substance of creation.

He's not talking about the feminine side as in a woman; he's talking about the feminine side as in the whole of Creation. He says that it is the nature of the feminine side to produce more of itself; more of its own attributes; more of its own essence. He says that the balance today on Earth is off because the feminine side is not producing more of itself, and this imbalance is being mirrored in nature...

Joseph takes over fully at this point: ...where you will find that soon there will be an imbalance in forthcoming generations, because whatsoever mankind believes as a whole is reflected in the nature around mankind, and there is a belief at the moment that the feminine side is not to be embraced and nurtured; is not to provide the function that it is there to provide.

Therefore, there is an imbalance in thinking; there is an imbalance in the grouping of souls at the moment, in the relationships between souls, because of the tendency of mankind – the feminine half of mankind – not to want to reproduce itself.

This goes against God's plan for the feminine aspect. The feminine aspect has to reproduce itself; the masculine aspect has to solidify, to stabilise itself. The masculine side is the stabilising influence, the feminine side is the reproductive influence, and **each growing soul contains within it a need and a desire to balance its masculine and feminine sides.**

I talked about the reasons for wars and upset on Earth the last time we spoke, but in addition to mankind's problems with the heart seed, there is also a problem with femininity. It is not being recognised, and this is leading to conflict, because the balance is not there and the feminine aspect is not recognising itself. You will, therefore, find that there is a greater predominance of feminine-related diseases and illnesses at the moment, because the feminine side is fighting itself and is not letting out its true nature.

What is the reason for there being a masculine and a feminine side to creation? The reason is that the subtle inter-penetration of these energies produces a specific field within which souls can evolve. So, the global masculine and feminine interplay in any one generation gives birth – literally – to a new set of circumstances, when balanced, for the next set of souls, for the next generation to experience. It is no coincidence that the new generation rebels against the current generation and looks back and says, 'The way that went before is not for us.' It's supposed to be that way, because the setup for each generation has to be different. Each generation of souls has to be born into a slightly different set of karmic conditions than the one that came before it. This is why your world progresses, makes breakthroughs in technology and in medicine through advances in scientific understanding. Each of these things comes about because of the interplay of male and female attributes which produce different sets of circumstances for progressive generations.

Now, if you take away either the influence of the masculine or of the feminine side you get an imbalance in the Field which the future generation must live in. You do not produce an ideal set of circumstances for the incoming set of souls, for the new generation, to evolve in. And this leads to upset; this leads to disillusionment for the souls of that new generation who are destined to live within that particular set of circumstances.

We are all inter-dependent and, yes, karma comes from God, and is placed around the soul when the soul incarnates but, because we are all inter-dependent, it is also down to the souls who come before to provide a way ahead for the next generation. And that is not happening – or it is not happening to the extent that it should. Prayers should be given out at this time for a healing of the feminine side, and the way to do this in advanced groups, as we do in our circles above yours, is to hold a bowl of water and, through imagination, to mix into that water silver light, then to send that silver light and water mix out in meditation as a ray into the consciousness of men and women. This has the effect of stimulating the feminine side of creation on Earth.

You've been taught many years ago, Michael, that the silver ray is a protective element and that that is its function as a part of the spiritual spectrum. It is, but it is also a *feminine* protective element, and I want you to consider tonight something that you've never considered before... **that wavelengths or vibrations are predominantly masculine or predominantly feminine**. Red, as you might expect, is a masculine element. Yellow is a feminine element. Blue is feminine. Silver is feminine. Mauve is an inter-penetration of the two. And so when we send out healing rays to people we are healing them not only with the colour, but also with either the masculine or feminine predominance of the coloured ray; because we wish the rays to harmonise with the organs in the physical body, which are also either predominantly masculine or predominantly feminine.

Consider the heart, which is equally balanced, which is why it has four chambers. The heart is equally balanced as a blend of masculine and feminine wavelengths. Now consider the liver... the liver is feminine. It may sound strange to you but the bowels have a particularly masculine resonance. The bones – the structure – are feminine, because the structure upholds the body and allows the body to move forwards. Anything that is a stabilising unit is predominantly masculine, anything that moves the body forwards, moves the body onwards – including the tear ducts – including the water supply through the body, is predominantly feminine. And so healers from our side send out a charge of energy as a coloured ray, but that ray also contains within it a masculine or feminine charge, which is what the organs we are attempting to heal need.

I mentioned the moon earlier. You say 'Mother Earth', but that is a misnomer. The predominant charge of the Earth is masculine. The predominant charge of the Moon, which is concerned with movement and the tides, is feminine. And there is a balance between the two with an ebb and flow to maintain the balance between masculine and feminine.

What I would ask you to do is look at objects over the next time period – before we meet again – and decide by holding them and looking at them whether they have a masculine or a feminine charge. And what I would ask you to do in your prayers is also to send out silver light, to have a water element close to you, to send out silver light and pray that the balance on Earth be healed at the moment, because it needs to be healed.

This topic concerns thinking as well, because thoughts can be masculine or feminine. This is nothing to do with the sex of the person who is thinking those thoughts. There are positive charges, there are negative charges; there are masculine charges and feminine charges to thoughts. All healing has a feminine charge because it is nurturing; whereas all ritual, all mediumship – whether it comes from a man or a woman – is a masculine charge.

Day and night have a masculine or a feminine charge, and it might surprise you to learn that the day is masculine and the night is feminine. The night is a nurturing time, it is a grouping time, it is a time when things can recover and move forwards, so it is feminine.

The universe is masculine and feminine, and always these two forces are trying to balance each other, and, of course, you will know that a soul, as it evolves, is trying to balance the masculine and the feminine forces within itself, trying to find an exact balance. For this reason, too, it is important that the world is balanced, which it is not at the moment.

Your weather is masculine and feminine. The Sun is a masculine element, whereas the rain and the winds and the clouds are feminine, because they provide growth, they provide nurturing for the future.

I – *Joseph* – am both masculine and feminine, and have, through many lifetimes, experienced elements of both, both as a man and as a woman, but now I choose to come through to you as a male. I am, however, (I hope, I pray to God!) a balance of both elements. And that balance, in my case, can be seen, again at my heart-centre, as a green tinge that is around the nested colours of the circle of my heart-centre when I choose to show (if you will forgive the pun) my *true colours*.

The feminine aspect of creation is, to my mind (although they are both equal) the most important; because men stand still and women go forwards, which is a contradiction to how you see things on Earth. Women go forwards because they produce the next generation, because they produce the thoughts that go into the heads of the next generation, whereas men – the masculine aspect – actually work with what is available now.

The feminine aspect plans for what is to come, and it is very sad to see that so many women have chosen to abandon that sacred trust and to stand still. They do not acknowledge that they are the creative force...

So, in this first discussion on creation I wanted to touch on the feminine side. I will touch on the masculine side next time.

My masculine side salutes you, my feminine side salutes you; and I pray that you are blessed in your attempts to integrate the two within yourselves.

Michael: He's gone...

Chapter Twelve
The Male Principle

Michael's observations: *Where am I going? What am I here for?* Aren't these questions each of us asks ourselves at some stage in our lives? Isn't the possibility of finding answers to these questions, in part, what attracted you to this book in the first place? In this communication, a companion to chapter 11, and in discussing the Male Principle, Joseph gives us a greater insight into who we are, but also majors on the amazing things we are and will eventually be capable of. The conclusions are quite shocking but also extremely uplifting.

Joseph: Sorry for the delay. I have been attempting to manipulate Michael, as some of the other guides have recently, so that I can get better involved with less interruption in what I want to say. [*Michael: Joseph is here referring to me again and increasingly being 'overshadowed' whilst sitting for communication – a process which could be described, I suppose, as a 'trance light' state, and, as I've mentioned* *previously, involving the guide who wishes to communicate coming very close to the medium and the medium surrendering a greater portion of his individual awareness, allowing the guide to take better control of the proceedings and speak more directly to the persons listening to the communication. Joseph's reference to 'with less interruption' makes me laugh, as it refers to my mind's wanting to comment at times on what is coming through whilst it is 'delivering' the information. It is amusing to me that the medium through which the communication takes place can, on occasion, be the 'interrupter' of that information.]*

So, first of all, a very good afternoon to you all; my Light be with you, my brightness be with you, my thoughts be with you, at this special time of year for the people on Earth. [*Michael: this communication was delivered just before Christmas, 2006.*]

I would like to begin by talking today about the Male Principle, as I promised I would a few weeks ago.

So, to recap, the Feminine Principle – the feminine energy – is concerned with growth and movement and, to some extent, the chaos that creates growth; and with the outgoing of energy, and the outpouring of energy, and an energetic strength that is mostly used 'behind the scenes'. The Feminine Principle is a hugely creative force, yet to observe women and girls on Earth at this moment, you would think that there is no such energy within them. Nevertheless, their souls have that potential. It is not being realised at the moment, but it is there. I would describe the Feminine Principle at the moment as being hidden, as being behind the scenes; as being, perhaps, dormant.

The Male Principle has also undergone change, and is struggling to express itself correctly in your current age.

The Male Principle dominates unchanging circumstances. The Male Principle is a foundation stone. The Male Principle builds and preserves ways of thinking. Certain vibrational clusters, certain vibrational ideals are brought forward by the Female Principle and are then built upon, founded, preserved, protected, by the Male Principle.

The Male Principle, the male vibration, is one of drawing in. The female vibration gives out; the male vibration draws in and solidifies. So, the male seeks to draw to himself everything that will complete – as he sees it – his life and his purpose.

You may say that men have always been warriors and have always been soldiers and have travelled abroad, but they do this in order to track down what they want and to bring it back to their point of origin.

So, the Male Principle – despite men being explorers, scientists and soldiers – always has that subconscious desire to gather in what it finds and what it discovers; to protect it; it is a protection principle. So many of the things that the Male Principle goes after are feminine in vibration, but the overriding instinct of the male vibration is to gather in those things, those Feminine Principles, and to fence them in, to consolidate them, to keep them unchanging.

The two need to be in harmony; the feminine to expand, the male to draw in; so that *temporary arrangements of matter can be created*, can be visualised, can be brought into form, as a result of male and female operating together.

The Male Principle needs to renew itself more than the Female Principle does. The Male Principle will apply itself to temporary arrangements, and will protect them and guard them with all its power, all its energy; **but things *must* change**, and it is the Female Principle within the structure of the Male Principle that brings that change, so that eventually things are torn down and the Male Principle has to renew itself, review its purpose, its intentions, and then, in conjunction with the Female Principle, it can create something new.

One force is expansive, one force is restrictive, and when the two forces are brought together, when they work as intended, they create new concepts, new ideas, new institutions, new ways of thinking, new political machines, new ideologies, new *civilisations*. Civilisation is born, culture is born, through that interplay between the Male and Female Principles; but always to eventually be torn down, and it is always the Female Principle that tears things down, that sweeps through the solidity and unchanging-ness of the Male Principle to bring about new form.

But there is much more to the Male Principle than simply holding onto ideas, because the Male Principle is linked into what has gone before, whereas the Female Principle is linked into what is to come.

With the Male Principle you have this solidity that is linked to the past. The Male Principle always builds on what has gone before, draws on that memory, draws on those vibrations. The Female Principle seeks always to expand and to change. And you take what has gone before, and you take the potential of what is to come, and by bringing them together you form *The Now*. That is how *The Now* is formed, by the balance of male and female energies.

If one is stronger than the other, then things are thrown out of balance. If there is too much feminine energy in an institution, it will very quickly destroy itself. If there is too much male energy in a concept, in a project, it will go nowhere, and, again, will just ruin itself. There has to be that balance.

At the moment in your world there isn't that balance. At the moment there is a dominance of the female energy, not only in females, but also in this generation – the upcoming generation – of males, because they have been taught to think in the female way, and this is causing imbalances at all levels. It is causing imbalances in relationships because there is no consolidation, there is only this desire to move onwards always, because of the dominance of the female energy.

So you have divorce, you have separation, you have a moving outwards from relationships which are doomed from the start because they do not strive for the balance of the Male and Female Principles within them.

If you contemplate global projects, there is much said but little done presently, because there is not the consolidation of the Male Principle being put into projects, into care of the planet, into the care of its peoples, into plans for the future, into solidifying those plans through action. And so positive concepts slip away and are lost...

You can see it in your own country in your lack of government. Words are spoken but nothing is done. Your country slips because it has slid into a dominance of the Female Principle.

This cannot be allowed to continue. Things have to change, or you will generate only apathy via the male vibration. There will be continued expansion of the female energy but nothing to expand, no new ideas, no consolidation of ideals to build on. No past from which to build a present. Nothing that has gone before – that is worthy – to push ahead with. *There has to be balance.*

You were created as souls to inhabit – during this lifetime on Earth – either a male or a female body; to explore the possibilities of the Male or the Female Principle... and the move away from this and into apathy and the move into a restless thinking of, 'Well, what am I? Am I male? Am I female? Does it matter?' is causing chaos.

There has to be regulation; there has to be a glorification of what God intended the soul to be during each incarnation. If it is male, it should celebrate and explore its maleness. If it is female, it should celebrate and explore its femininity. I am not talking about trans-sexual states nor the apparent gender of the physical body. I am not talking about what some on Earth call aberrations, which are *not* aberrations. I am talking about the soul exploring the range of vibrations that it has come here to explore. If it has come here to be male, let it be male; if it has come here to be female, let it be female.

Your animals have no such problems, your animals know their roles as souls instinctively. But there is a big problem with identity, with soul-identity, at the moment. It is symptomatic of a problem I mentioned earlier, this being that souls seek to enjoy this incarnation again and again and again, with no responsibilities, always seeking the experience of the incarnation for sensual reasons. No! You are part of the ecology; you are here to create the background for the next generation of souls. What background? What is being created? Certainly not anything with permanence.

The Principles are out of control. I would ask that you pray – when you pray to God – that people seek to identify themselves, seek to remember who they are, why they are here, the roles they are supposed to play, because eventually the soul reaches a state – as I have reached a state – where it is aware that it is neither male nor female, but that it is both.

And the greatest expressions of the soul – when it reaches my level – are brought about through balance.

We create. We create science by projecting from the balance of our souls... by, in your terms, bringing into being concepts, looking at them and seeing if they work. If they don't, we accentuate the female aspect to take away what we have created, and then we create anew until something is to our liking, until something feels to be in harmony with the God within us. But we can only do this by having the balanced tool of creation within ourselves, that balance of male and female. We are neither one thing nor the other at this stage. Male and female are attributes, are factors we can bring out of our souls.

And you will recognise in what I am saying – particularly the lady [*Michael: Joseph is referring to Jane here*] – that I am talking about, in male and female, the polarities of negative and positive. So everything I have said about male and female can be applied to negative and positive forces. We are balancing these, and there is much need for balance in your world, for you to begin balancing them too.

So the Male Principle – ideally – is a principle that seeks to encompass, to encircle the Feminine Principle to stop it expanding, and when it cannot expand further it mixes with the Male Principle and creates *structure*. That structure is then in place as long as the Male Principle is dominant.

Inevitably the Male Principle in any structure – be it an idea, an institution, an object… whatever it is – the Male Principle decays, becomes weaker, lets out the Female Principle which becomes stronger and the object, the ideal, the structure is destroyed. And then the process starts again.

So, male and female are ciphers for positive and negative, and in learning to balance male and female and understand male and female we are understanding positive and negative, the construction and the deconstruction of form and of matter, which is vitally important.

In your world when you want something you are used to going out and buying it. It is there; it is packaged; it is ready. Someone else has made it for you. Your ultimate destiny as a Proto-God, however, *is to make it for yourself.*

Initially, on Earth, you take wood and nails, and steel and machines, and you make something. Then, as you progress when you are on the lower levels of the spirit-worlds you begin to bring images – creations – into your life, with help from others. As you progress further those images and those creations take on more complexity, more significance, until you can eventually create a new world, a new star.

You are Proto-Gods.

You have that potential… but you are presently on the lowest rung of the ladder. You are at a point where you do not even recognise that, within you, you have the tools and everything you need to create.

Am I describing myself as a God? Yes, but you are too! Children of God! At this time of year [*Michael: Christmas time*] do you not say *The Son of God*? Understand the real meaning of this: **YOU are a son, a daughter of God.**

Your potential is there, within you now. Within your soul at this moment you have all the components to create whatever you want, and as you progress that ability to create grows. At first you will do it in groups. At first it will take a number of individuals – of souls – to create something. Imagine your delight, for example, in bringing forth a bolt of cloth; in joining with other people to create it mentally, not having to weave it or to grow the material, just bringing it forth; and that is just a simple matter. You are destined to create far more than a bolt of cloth, because the Creator, step by step, is showing you His ways, His abilities, and showing you not only what He can do but that He has given you the ability to do it too. It starts with balance in all things.

Perhaps I have gone a little further than usual today, but the gift I would like to give you at this special time is the acknowledgement, the understanding of your limitless capability. There are many who feel that, yes, there is life after death; yes, souls must go on; but they think always of the human form, they think always of a safe place with houses and streets and things they are familiar with, but this is such a small corner of Creation. There is so much more for you; and, yes, you will be a human, and, yes, you will remember and manifest this form as I am doing now. But it is not your true form, and to think that your destiny as a species is to get up and go to work and worry about coupons and comestibles and competition between you for things that are transient is so heartbreaking. The minute you leave those things behind in your lives you become truly creative.

So with the three of you, [*Michael: myself, Jane and David*] *create* your lives from now on. We are pleased to see new ventures begin, but share in that creation, shake off what has gone before, realise your potential. Use the Male and Female Principles to create on behalf of others. That is the greatest gift you have been given.

Chapter Thirteen
Light

Michael's observations: This was a further pre-Christmas session, and one which came about quite unexpectedly as I sat in Peter's office with Peter and Jane. I include Joseph's comments to Peter at the end of this chapter because they contain words of wisdom that are relevant to us all.

Joseph: First of all, thank you for putting aside the physical world for the amount of time it will take us to commune on a spiritual level with you. It is very important that people do this, but not many people do. Not many people, for the good of their own souls, put aside five or ten minutes each day in order to commune with the higher side of their being. I am, in effect, the higher side of your being, because I am a spirit who is linked to you, and who is speaking to you from a higher level of evolution.

Where you sit today, I once sat, although not in such luxurious style! And we are one organism. We are linked so that you can listen to the higher mind. I am also listening to the higher mind, because I am listening to the people – the souls – 'above' me, who are talking to me and who are listening to the souls 'above' them, and we are all listening to the God-mind, which is the highest form of creative process, as we bring through the information you are recording now.

I want to talk to you today about Light and its properties and qualities. Light is motion. Light is a journey. Light is the exuding, the putting-forth, of energy from the Godhead. Light isn't still, as you will know from physics. Light moves, and Light, moving through bodies, through objects, changes them. Light is also an expression of the mental, loving process of God, so the quality of the Light we give out is an expression of God's intention and our intentions – as spirits – towards an object or a person.

What I mean by that is that different frequencies and harmonies of Light can be sent to and *through* a person on Earth, because Light never stays around a person, it goes to them and through them; it travels onwards so that certain conclusions can be brought about by its interaction with other souls as it expands outwards from its source, the God-centre. *Light reaches its primary target then continues to do good.*

In healing, varying levels of Light are sent to people. Vibrations of Light – different wavelengths of Light – are sent to people so that the trash, the rubbish, the vibrations those souls have accumulated and don't need, can be taken away from them.

Because Light, of course, is able to penetrate darkness, we use various frequencies of Light to get rid of the darker vibrations that surround and penetrate people. We then use certain other frequencies of Light to heal the physical object (the body); and another frequency of Light to heal the mental object (the mind); and another frequency of Light to heal the psychic object, the spiritual object (the soul and the spirit). If you were to watch us transmitting Light, it would seem to you as though different colours of Light were hitting the person we were directing it to. Each of those streams, each of those frequencies, has a job to do.

Some of them remove matter, remove vibrations. Some of them encourage organs to re-grow, or to heal themselves... 'regenerate' is the word I'm looking for. Some of them penetrate the mental field and separate from that mental field some of the negative thoughts the person has picked up about themselves which they believe to be true, and which are making them ill. So, we sever the connection between the thoughts and the person so that the person can look at those thoughts objectively and think, 'I don't need those any more.' They can then let go of them; they can let them fade away.

Other vibrations of Light stimulate the spirit; stimulate the soul, because the strength within any healing operation has to come from a belief within the soul being healed that everything is well once again, that everything is healed. So, we send out multi-rays of Light to heal all aspects of the person receiving the healing. How do we do this? We sit together in a circle, or as a band of souls, and each of us concentrates on one of those wavelengths of Light, concentrating that Light towards the person or persons who are doing the healing – the healer on the physical plane. In turn they then pass on, send out from their solar plexus that Light which affects the person on Earth who requires healing.

But we don't just use Light for healing purposes; we also use it for teaching purposes, and you've been told in one of the recordings you made earlier that we use a ray of Light in order for me to speak through Michael and to bridge the gap between the two of us in terms of distance and evolution, to result in speech you can understand on this level.

So, we use Light for communication as well. **Light *is* communication**. Whenever you send out Light to someone you are communicating *love* to them. If you want to pray effectively, send out Light to someone... don't ask for someone to get better in a certain way, or for them to think a certain thing, or to act in a certain way, **simply send them Light**.

If you sit down and think of a person who needs healing, very often your guide will place a colour into your mind so that you can send out that colour vibration to the person you are thinking about, and that will do much more good than your saying, 'Father, I want x, y and z [*to happen to somebody*]', because you don't know what the ultimate purpose is in their suffering. If you send out Light, pure and simple Light, you are reinforcing the God within them, so whatever the reason that that suffering is there with them for, it will be transmuted, it will be helped along, it will be *lightened* – even if it is a karmic lesson they are going through – by the Light that you send to them.

We are all Light-givers. We are all Light-bringers, and Light is what the world needs, not as some phrase – not as some cliché – but as a fact.

The world needs Light.

Having to penetrate the darkness of your world is like trying to open a clamshell. It is like trying to take a crowbar to a chest that is deep underground or underwater, because the vibrations that surround you are so murky and so heavy, and only a small portion of what we try to get through to you succeeds in getting through at all. So, we have to penetrate the murkiness of your level of consciousness with Light and, again, we band together to do this, forming a chain of Light linked to other spheres. Souls who are 'above' us in the higher spheres channel Light 'down' to us and we draw in this God-Light and send it towards the Earth – as we are sending it towards Michael now – so that you can hear me and so that we can penetrate that dark vibration. People who are 'below' us – although 'below' is a misnomer... people who are not yet at our evolutionary level yet living in spiritual dimensions... also channel Light on our behalf, receiving it as we send it to them, then channelling it down towards the Earth plane.

Your lives should not be as they are. Your lives should be blissful, carefree opportunities to grow and to learn, exercises in understanding who you are, in understanding your spirit and the nature of the God within you.

It is the accumulated psychic and mental debris of millions of souls created, imagined, over thousands and thousands of years that pushes you down. You are born into a world that already has an opinion about you from the first second that you draw breath. And that opinion is that you are doomed to fail. That opinion is that you are doomed to grow old. That opinion is that you cannot succeed in anything that you do, and that you have to work, you have to toil, you have to struggle, you have to be in pain, and you believe all this because you are surrounded by a field of negative consciousness which suffers from an absence of Light.

So, our task is to bring Light to the world. Jesus said, 'I am the Light of the World.' Why do you think he said this? He wasn't describing himself. He was describing the God within him and within us all. *I am* God. *I am* the Light of the World.

In connecting with God we bring Light into this world, we bring Light into the darkness, and that is our task. You wonder sometimes about how accurate you are in receiving the information that comes through from us, but as long as the communication comes through as Light that you can pass onto someone else, don't even worry about the words. It is the motive; it is the Light that is important. If you take a taper and you light one candle, and then another, and then another, the light grows, and that is our purpose in communicating with you; to light more candles, to have more people capable of going from one to another and leaving Light within those they meet, so that finally we can penetrate this wall of disbelief and remind people of who they are.

If you take away the shared Field of consciousness on Earth, if you take away the darkness, then the soul begins to remember that it itself is Light! If we were to strip away your physical body, if we were to strip away your mental body, if we were to strip away your astral body, what would we be left with? We would be left with consciousness that is embedded within a spark, within *Light*.

The God that people seek in religion, in churches, in kneeling, in clasping their hands and closing their eyes, and saying, 'Where are you, God?' is within them all the time. It's *Light*, but they will never realise this until sufficient Light is brought back into this world, and I say *back* because your world has gone into a decline, and there was a time when there was sufficient

Light on Earth for people to know who they were and to live accordingly.

'The Fall' is a story that I will tell you one day – how that happened. How your world became as it is now. For now it is sufficient for you to know that a 'fall' from grace, if you like, from illumination, *did* happen, and that this world wasn't scheduled to be the dark place that it is today. And it amuses me to see your television advertising for Christmas that is all baubles and light and people getting this and people getting that, and not one of those presents will truly bring Light to anyone receiving them unless the person who sends them out has first enveloped them in Light. And then the present is not the present sent, but it is the Light within the present sent, and that is the true present, the true gift from the heart.

What can you give someone *truly* that will lift them up? Light! Nothing else, because that is what they are, that is all there is, in God-reality, and that is what they truly need.

We look forward to a time when people sit together on Earth to produce a sea of Light that can then be sent out across your world to help wherever help is needed; a time when hospitals will have people surrounding them with Light, and will have rooms where people – Light-workers – are able to come and sit with people to bathe those suffering souls, those patients, in Light. You invade the physical body and think that you can cure something. What can you cure? You are taking a scalpel – which itself is an illusion – and you are cutting the body – which itself is an illusion – and taking out something that is also an illusion. What can you heal? You can only heal with *Light*. You can only heal by putting a hand on the head of the person and saying, 'Be still... everything is fine. You are a part of God. You can never die. You are loved. You are going somewhere. You are evolving.

You are part of us... there is no need to fear.' ...And in doing that, you heal.

All problems come from the feeling of separation. To set boundaries based on the extremities, the physical limits, of the physical body – to believe that *This is me; that is not me...* is to believe in an illusion. Better to say, 'This is me; that is *also* me... I affect the Field. I am part of the Field. I am part of you. You are part of me. You are my brother. You are my sister.' Light is needed to make people realise these basic spiritual truths.

I would talk of crime as well, because what do you do with your criminals? We understand your reaction, but you lock them away and you then feed them with your thoughts of darkness so that they become more like the people you expect them to be, not less. Light transforms people. Something we never do from this side is judge anyone... and your hardened criminals, your rapists, your murderers... we send them Light, because one day they will stand where I am standing, and one day those memories of what they have done will have helped to propel them forwards into my sphere; in ways that we can't explain to you at this point, but will in another communication.

The world is given opportunities every day to love, but it prefers instead to hate. Souls are given opportunities to love people in hospitals, opportunities to love people in prisons, opportunities to love people within their family circles, and opportunities to love themselves... to bring through Light, and they ignore them.

So, to distil what I am talking about today, the greatest weapon for good that can ever be used is *Light*. We use it all the time. I myself am a vibration of Light. I choose to come through to you with a human form, but that human form is an illusion.

It is a 'hologram'. It is a projection of Light in a certain way that gives me the appearance of human form.

And there are planets in this physical universe on which beings of Light live in a far different way than you do. They are as far away from you in thought and approach to life as you are from some of your microbes. And yet there is no real difference between them and you, except in their ability to accept, to live within, the Light.

So, your mission, your job, is to bring Light to your world, whether you use that Light in the way you speak to comfort someone, or whether you use that Light to diffuse an argument between two people, or whether it is a matter of you sending out Light to the other side of the world to help with conditions there, or of giving yourself Light, of clearing your head.

Do you know what 'clearing your head' means from a spiritual point of view? Clearing your head means getting rid of the negative, the darker vibrations you have accrued over the years and saying, 'There is nothing wrong... there is only Light. Now I can think straight because there is only Light.'

That's why we come to you, to bring you Light, and all of my communications can be distilled to that one point.

Now I have to go back to the Light, because working in conditions – even with people on my side who are enveloping me in Light so that I can communicate – working in conditions on the Earth plane is tiring. It is like being drained. It is like losing consciousness, but not going unconscious. It is like losing God-consciousness; which is the most precious thing we have, like losing – forgetting – my most precious connection to my God.

I have to go, but I can come back and I can talk on other topics; but before I do, I would like to talk very briefly to Peter and would say, *I am standing next to you.* I have my hand out. I am holding you by the shoulder, but because of the difference in our frequencies you cannot feel me... which is sad. I cannot prove to you that I am here, but I will endeavour, in the thoughts that come to you in coming months, to prove to you that I am around, because you will find yourself thinking in my way, or – as I do with Michael sometimes when he is walking down the street – I will give you a concept and you will think, 'I have never thought of it in that way before.' When that happens, it is not imagination, it is me.

Don't be so hard on yourself. Don't feel that you have looked in the wrong corners, because you haven't. Everything is a stepping-stone to everything else. Knowledge builds. Therefore, wherever you've looked, whatever you've done, you've been in the right place and you've learned the right things.

How many people do you think could sit in a room like this and listen to me? So many of them are so bowed down by the volume of greyness and darkness they have around them that they cannot. So congratulate yourself...

Michael: He's gone...

Chapter Fourteen
Atlantis and the Fall

Michael's observations: In perhaps one of the most important communications transcribed for Revelation, Joseph refers at some length to 'the Fall', a cataclysmic change of vibration that plunged the Earth and its peoples into a restrictive darkness from which we and the planet are still suffering (An entire volume devoted to the event, explaining its origins, the reasons for negativity and violence on Earth, and what is being done spiritually to change things was delivered in later communications and subsequently published as Joseph's fourth book, appropriately titled the Fall). In this chapter Joseph also reveals that he had once lived in what we would today term 'Atlantis', sharing a vision with me, as he spoke, of a beautiful city set against a lilac-coloured sky and surrounded by waters in which sailed majestic vessels (below and in future communications he invites us to challenge any ingrained preconceptions and/or biases regarding the term... in Trance Mission, for example – a record of his public trance demonstrations – he explains that the location was sited in 'a different vibration of the Earth plane than the one you are used to', further qualifying this by stating that ours is not the first civilisation to be here, and that others have risen and fallen in the distant past).

Joseph: I would like to talk today about emotions; about happiness; about sadness; about the motives behind emotions and about what emotions really are.

It may seem strange to you that the emotional 'package' that each human being is given when they incarnate on Earth is not what they actually are; it is *not* a part of their true spirit personality. Those earthly emotions exist to help them to deal with the karmic package that they are also given when they incarnate. In other words, if a person was emotionally neutral – if they did not react to karmic stimulus via the emotions they had been given – then the karmic situations unfolding around them would be dismissed by the person as unimportant. The challenges they presented would not be entered into wholeheartedly, albeit on a subconscious level, by the soul, and the karma would not be as effective in helping their soul to evolve. However, if the emotions are tailored to the working out of the individual's karma (which they are) then the person ultimately gets the most out of that karma by entering into the challenges from the standpoint of having those particular emotions, of responding to karmic circumstances from a particular emotional blend and bias. So, the karmic situations that come to people are formulated to impact upon, to work with, the emotional makeup of each person; no two people will react in the same way to a given set of karmic circumstances.

Before a person incarnates, the Lords of Karma – those spirits who determine the course of that soul's life, and how that life will link into the courses of other lives during its time on Earth – also determine where that soul would be best placed geographically in order to gain the emotional background it will need in order to grow.

A soul will be placed with a certain set of parents for many reasons, but the basic reason is to give that soul – through the exchange of parental DNA that puts together the physical body of that soul – the right equipment *emotionally* in order for it to gain the most from the karma that will come to it. I know that sounds a little complicated, but souls who come to Earth are far better equipped than they know *in every respect* to learn and to progress during the lifetime that they spend here.

All this is done so that the soul won't have to spend much time here, because the Earth is a dangerous plane; it has many pitfalls for evolving souls. It contaminates evolving souls, and so, if a soul wishes to come back to Earth – as so many do – that soul is given as much help as can possibly be given to it, in the name of love, from the higher spheres, so that it has the right emotional background, the right material background, and, of course, the right spiritual help. That soul can then, in one lifetime (if things go according to plan) evolve and take great strides in spiritual evolution. And it is always hoped that by the time a soul returns to the spirit world – gets back home – it will have decided that it now wants to move on and away from the Earth.

The reason I am talking about emotions is to explain that there is a racial aspect to karma as well as an individual aspect. Certain races are imbued with certain sets of emotions. For example, Michael's father – of the Italian race – is highly emotional, is highly passionate, and those attributes, those aspects of that race, have been mixed into Michael's karmic situation, and into his mediumship situation, so that he can get the most out of both. Souls are placed within certain races for a reason. By mixing the attributes of certain races you set up the circumstances in which the next generation can thrive spiritually – can change through the karma that comes to them – so the racial placing of a soul on Earth is a very intricate affair.

I want to talk further about the Lords of Karma. These great spirits, sometimes mentioned in spiritual circles, *do* exist. They are souls who have become – as a result of countless incarnations and countless experiences – almost an elite, although 'elite' is the wrong word when talking about spiritual matters. These souls have evolved to a point where they have been given custody of certain souls 'under' them in the name of love. A sphere exists here that is inhabited by the Lords of Karma, whose grave mission it is to place souls in the circumstances where they can grow the most, both on Earth and on other worlds, in other spheres.

These spirits, in conjunction with the God that they have grown closer to through experience, the God they can listen to much more easily from within as a result of their long spiritual evolution, and in conjunction with the angelic spheres, determine where each evolving soul should go. They sit in conference; they sit in council, and they plot out the proposed life of each soul. They get the background right. They place the soul within certain races and with certain parents so that the soul can obtain the correct emotional attributes it needs during that lifetime. They then have to negotiate 'pathways' so that each soul meets the other souls and circumstances they are supposed to meet during their incarnation; so there is a complexity in that they are placing souls with parents, but they are also plotting 'points', from your point of view, ahead of that soul, to make sure that the soul reaches certain cycles, certain milestones, certain key points in its life. You can appreciate the incredible complexity of what they are doing, and such is their dedication that they have very little time for themselves as spirits; they are constantly in communication with the God-within, with the angelic hosts, and with each other in plotting the lives of souls on Earth and in other spheres.

Descending from them you then have further councils in other spheres of lesser vibration, who watch over each soul, who try, who attempt – the soul's life path having been set up by the Lords of Karma – to keep it running on the right set of rails, so that it will arrive at the other key points in its life. And then, descending from these councils, you have the guides who talk to you regularly to nudge you in certain directions.

I know that it has been said that everything is happening *now*, and it is; this is all part of the map I often talk about. The Lords of Karma have, if you like, the ultimate 'map of the soul'.

Sometimes, because of the complexity of what they do, mistakes are made, and souls miss key points and miss connections. This rarely happens, but sometimes it does happen because so much has to be observed constantly for the benefit of each incarnated soul. Now when this happens there is the question of karma, as the karma will not then unfold around that soul as it was originally intended to. At the end of its life on Earth there will be a dispensation for such a soul because its karma has been altered – not by that soul, but by a missed opportunity, by an opportunity that has been overlooked by the Lords of Karma.

The analogy I would like to bring to you is that of the ladies on Earth who worked during the Second World War to move around, in a map room, clusters of model aircraft, and to report back to those in higher authority, who would then make decisions based upon where the real counterparts of those aircraft were. That is what the Lords of Karma and the guides under them do. Their sphere is a gigantic 'map-room', if you will, with each soul's life being plotted within it.

Why is it so important, why is so much care taken over the life – the earthly existence, or the existence in another sphere – of each soul? Because God wills it for one thing, and because karma is designed to gradually extricate each soul from the darkness that it finds itself in.

We have talked for months about souls 'going home', going back to God, which they eventually do, but now into the mix we have the information that the Persian Gentleman has given you about the Fall.*

You now know that souls that exist on the Earth plane are advancing themselves spiritually but are also working out group karma or racial karma that goes back millennia. But God is fair. God gives each soul the ultimate chance to come back to Him and will not rest until each of His Children is back home. So, the karma is worked out to give each soul the optimum opportunity to extricate itself from the lessons of the past that are still being learned and to work out its own personal karma so that it can move forwards in the scheme of things. This is what the phrase, 'the sins of the fathers are visited on the sons', actually means.

The sins of the fathers are visited on the sons... It is the acts of those souls such a long, long time ago, that plunged the consciousness of those souls into darkness, that are still being

---

* 'The Persian Gentleman' is our name for another of our guides.

worked out.

I have to say that this is not a punishment from God. Those souls separated themselves from God because their vibrations differed. God did not cast them out, they cast themselves out. And they cast themselves out of the paradise – the Garden of Eden – that this planet originally was. Therefore God, in compassion, has, since that time, attempted to reach out to those souls and bring them out of their self-imposed darkness.

Many of the key figures around the world who cause so much destruction and chaos, many of the world leaders who appear to be – in your terms – evil, are members of those original soul groups that became 'lost' so long ago.

So, when you see great cataclysms, when you see people who appear to be causing so much chaos, it is because they are being given an opportunity. At any time during such a life they can change. At any time they can say, 'This is wrong. I'm going to stop doing this... I'm going to evolve. I'm going to turn to the Light. I can see the error of my ways.' Few of them do, but again and again they are given opportunities to do so. And you will find that many of these people rise into powerful positions today because originally, millennia ago, they held powerful positions. Originally there were many souls under their jurisdiction, under their 'love', their guidance; and when that guidance became corrupted, the souls that were under that guidance were also 'punished' in a way, because of that change in vibration. Instead of loving the souls in their care they controlled them, they dishonoured them.

The Earth is working its way back to the paradise that it once was, and the souls that are on the Earth are a mixture. Some of them are souls that have been linked to the Earth for thousands and thousands of years, who go back to the time of the Fall, who were once beings of Light and will be again one day. And there is an input of 'newer', uncontaminated souls, but the Earth, as we have said in previous lectures, has a pull, a temptation; it is a place that souls feel compelled to revisit and revisit and revisit, to re-enter the chaos, to relive the chaos, because there is still an echo from the Fall. There is still that magnetic pull, that temptation from the time when things went wrong; from the time when the Light was all but extinguished, and souls who come here as 'new' souls, as uncontaminated incarnations of God to reveal the Light, are quite brave, and many of them become 'lost'. This is why the Guidance Network, this is why the Lords of Karma exist, to extricate those souls and to eventually bring back the original souls into the fold.

I know that this sounds biblical, but the story of the Fall has its basis in truth. It is a race memory. What I am saying to you should resonate with you as truth, because it *is* truth. And every soul knows in its heart, because every soul is part of God, that there was a time when things were different here, when things were better on the Earth.

We have to bring every soul to the point where it chooses *not* to come back here, where it chooses other levels of evolution, so that the Earth can rest, so that it can lay fallow for a time and then be restored to its former glory.

There have been other civilisations. I was part of one. I was linked with Atlantis. I am showing Michael now a vision of buildings and a seashore and the mountains that were part of a city I visited many times. We had a different technology than you have at the moment. We used particle physics to move objects. We had transportation systems that were not based on crude mineral oils. We were able to move and to rearrange buildings with our minds. We were able to heal people without touching them. We were able to place into objects power, the power of Light, so that we had instruments that could build things if we concentrated on them – tools that you would not understand today, because your tools today are based upon material things only; you never incorporate spiritual elements into material objects. We did.

...We did...

Our emphasis was on the spiritual side. We had Light-energy that didn't require electricity. We had halls of thought that people could visit to contemplate the situations in their lives, to grow in education, to grow in knowledge and experience; and we had a system that was not based on a government, because a government implies that you are overshadowing people, that you are telling them what to do. There was true democracy. Those who were less able were cared for; those who could not contribute to society were, nevertheless, fed and clothed and given shelter. I know it sounds as though I am describing Utopia but such was our civilisation.

This was around the time of the Fall; this was around the time when the only difference in souls was that it was very evident with physical eyes that some men and women were very advanced souls; and they were benevolent, and they would visit us and they would bring us information about God and Creation.

And then the seductive nature of being able to create and to change physical matter changed these people. It didn't change us, but it changed them; and I can only describe it as a submergence of thought. There was a lot of pain, there was a lot of death, which was caused by these people suddenly creating dark things, dark thoughts that previously didn't exist on the Earth. It changed the nature of how animals looked at each other, and the vibrations were absorbed by the flora and fauna. The Earth became a more aggressive place.

Our civilisation disappeared – not in my time – but shortly after I had departed for the spirit worlds, and the knowledge was lost; the ability to work with Light – the ability to blend and work with matter and Light – was lost, and has still not been rediscovered.

The generations that followed suffered greatly because they had no knowledge of God. They had wrapped themselves up in total illusion, and cut themselves off from their own souls; and there followed a very materialistic time. And for a time souls were in limbo. There were no human souls on this planet, and that is the gap that you see, that you regard as history. You regard history as starting with some forms of life and man coming to be, but man came to be for the *second time*. Such was the darkness that was around the Earth that there had to be a period during which plans, if you like, were formulated as to how to move the souls that had placed themselves in darkness. They were put to sleep, they had no knowledge of time having passed, of experience having passed; but then, slowly, the Earth was repopulated, and into the mix of souls that were incarnating onto the planet were then introduced some of those that were in darkness; only slowly at first. And it took many lifetimes for them to come out of that darkness.

This, I hope, explains why there has been such violence in your history, because the violence comes from the struggles of the souls that 'fell', trying to make sense of who they were; trying, with the help of the Lords of Karma, to come out of that darkness, and for many, many years, always choosing bloodshed and violence instead.

The Earth stands poised for a time of Light, for a time of spiritual enlightenment, but this will not be without cataclysms; and the cataclysms I am talking about are of a natural order, rather than being of a man-made nature. There will be vast changes to the Earth over the next sixty years or so, but as a result of that this time of peace, this time of love, *will* come.

The plan is, then, that the planet will be populated by people who are spiritually minded, who will rediscover something of what can be done with Light; the construction, the sculpting, the changing of matter through the use of God-Light, and then, at that point, when the planet has become 'Christed' (and this will not happen in sixty years, this will take much longer than that) the souls that still lie sleeping will be brought out of that darkness. The remaining, if you like, God-men that people talk about, God-men and women who fell, will be brought out of the darkness and the purpose of the planet will then be wound up, and new creative spheres will be brought forth.

I still create in my sphere of existence the backdrop of my background, the Earth that I knew that is vastly different from the Earth that you know. You feel there are changes through global warming, but I tell you that the Earth as you see it now is just a pale shadow of how it used to look, of the beauty this world once had. And thought – mistaken thought – has done all that, has caused the havoc, the chaos. But I choose to go down to my seashore and I choose to look out at the hills and to recreate part of the city that I knew so well, because it gives me great comfort.

And I am talking to you at a distance, which is why it is always difficult for Michael to link to me for long periods of time. Not a distance in terms of miles that can be measured with a ruler, but a distance in terms of evolution. You and I are separated by a great deal of evolution, spiritually-speaking.

I was around a long time ago, as you would understand it. My thinking is different from yours, which is why I have had to learn, to study, in order to talk to you. My stature is different than yours. Michael says that I am short, but I was of normal height for my race. And I am showing Michael now what I am wearing, or what I would have worn, and he can see that, woven into what are metal strands – but not as you would understand them – is Light; we clothed ourselves in Light. It was a true paradise; it was the paradise that is spoken about in many ancient texts.

So, I hope that I have illuminated you, and that amuses me, because we have been talking about Light, with regard to what has happened before on this world. It is an arrogance to suppose that your people are the first people; that your civilisation is the first civilisation. It is not.

Many of our artefacts have been found but have not been understood, because they do not resemble yours. Going back to the time of Egypt, the time of Rome, that is not the beginning of great civilisation.

And there have always been seers who could connect with the true antiquity of civilisation, who have been able to bring through some of our knowledge, but it is time that the Earth woke up, time that it realised that mistakes had been made before and could be made again.

We want an army of love, not an army of chaos; we want souls to be aware, not in darkness. And that is why I am communicating with you. We are the same. We are all Children of God. My soul has been coloured by my experiences, just as yours have; and I am from a different age, from a different possibility, and I do not want mankind to make the mistakes that it has made before. It seems at the moment to be sinking further into the dream, to be glorifying its technology that has no basis in Light; to be glorifying its medicine that seeks to corrupt creation, which is hell-bent – literally – on cloning, on experimentation, on changing the order of things physically; when, if it listened to its soul, its heart, it would see that this is not the right thing to do. Such experiments have taken place in the past with disastrous results.

So, our message – the reason why I have come back – is to make people stop and think; is to give them their soul history, and to awaken them to possibilities, and say, 'You are far more than you think you are.' Please do not be arrogant, please do not think you are the ultimate race, you are not. Mistakes have been made before and can be made again. There is a plan for this Earth, and it is a move towards the Light and not the darkness.

I have said enough for now.

My blessing on you; my peace and love be with you, and be assured that one day we will meet to discuss this when you have passed from (and I have to say it) this 'veil of tears'.

Chapter Fifteen
Work

Michael's observations: During this session Joseph revealed more about what we would term 'Atlantis' and the way in which his society worked. By this point David, Jane and myself had decided that we had a common goal, that of making available to as many people as possible as much channelled information from Joseph and our guides as we were able to bring through in our lifetimes. During the session, the second we had held in a single day in order to speed the production of this book, which Joseph was urging and eagerly anticipating, he gave us a title for our little group, which you will see printed on the cover of this book and on all subsequent publications: *The Band of Light*.

Joseph: I would like to talk to you this afternoon about the concept of work, and that concept I wish to divide into two categories: the first is how you occupy your time, and the second is **THE** work.

First of all, how you occupy your time: unfortunately, most occupations on the Earth plane are neither creative nor uplifting. Your society has created a need for drudgery in order that levels of materialism be maintained; and nothing destroys, nothing beats down the human spirit, more than drudgery.

You have heard many philosophies that suggest you should inject God-power into everything that you do, and these are very true, they are very sound. However, it is difficult for many people, once under that pall of drudgery, to expand their souls, to lift themselves up, and this is the fault of society rather than of the individual.

In my day each person was looked upon as a vital part of the whole. No one was treated differently than anyone else, and people were found work, a way to occupy their time, that uplifted their spirit and also contributed to society.

You have a great problem today with work, because as you think, so you are. If people are in occupations that pull them down, that give them no inspiration or hope, then those are the thoughts that emanate from those souls into the atmosphere, contributing to the depression, the darkness, the restrictiveness of this world by placing people in restrictive occupations.

I am not suggesting that the whole world should be creative, but I *am* suggesting that the attitude to work should be different, because the attitude to work is: *let us be as productive as possible in order to get as much mammon as possible*. If workloads were staggered, and people worked a day at a time then had a free day, then worked another day and had a free day, their spirits would have time to recover, and it would be better if the companies concerned – those companies which are responsible for creating such demeaning tasks, for placing such demeaning tasks in front of souls – sought to provide better conditions for the souls under their employ. The whole system you have at the moment is geared towards making more material things …faster and faster …more and more productive …more and more automated …more and more *boring* …and all this stifles the spirit.

Each soul is capable of creating in some way because each soul creates as a matter of course, being a part of God. I am not suggesting that you place a paintbrush in the hands of each person – that would be unproductive – but there is something creative that each soul can do. And if companies and corporations realised this and provided the tools for their workers to do something creative with, then their production would go up. However, they would find as this happened that they had been changed by the experience, and that they really didn't want to produce the goods they are now producing, because they would realise, in adopting a more spiritual approach, that those goods are too linked in with a material world. They would instead seek to produce something new and of more worth to a more spiritually-minded society.

Everything we had in Atlantis, the possessions we owned, were hand-crafted or thought-crafted. We had no factories, we had no production lines, and so every object produced was slightly different. You could have two objects with a similar function but they would be quite different, because they would reflect the personality of the souls that made them.

What I am attempting to explain is the soullessness of your world with regard to its material objects today. There is no love in them. There is no love in your television set or your car; there is no love in your furniture or your house – your purpose-built house – because the only love built into these objects is a love of the money that they will produce for someone. Your televisions would work more efficiently, your houses would be more welcoming, if they had love put into them at the design and creation stage; if a little time was taken over things, which it isn't.

And the speed at which souls work today prevents us from reaching them. The reason that Michael's life course – with regard to material work – is vastly different from most people's is so that he can provide time for us to communicate with him. There is no time for God in the lives of souls today. They work and they work and they work, and then they return to the spirit world – and then they often choose to return to the Earth plane to repeat the cycle!

Work is not all there is. Creativity is extremely important. We are not suggesting that a soul should do nothing, but for a soul, day in, day out, week in, week out, as the years go by, to be involved in something mindless, is as torturous to that soul as some of the cruelty inflicted on souls in times before this one. It is mental cruelty; it is physical cruelty. The soul always seeks to fly free and to grow, and your society will not allow that.

Work is important, yes, but what I would say to the people reading this book is *choose your work carefully*. Be at the centre of a balance, so that on the one side you have the work that is necessary for you to pay unto Caesar what is Caesar's, but on the other side you have creativity, you have time for your God, you have time to explore what your soul is capable of. Because in creating, whether it be a sculpture or a painting or growing a plant, you are exploring your God qualities. And your God qualities are your *good* qualities; they are always for the good. And the more people that balance their lives in this way, the brighter the Earth will become, and the freer the Earth will be from the negativity we have spoken about previously, from the evil that was originally done; from the 'original sin' if you like (sin meaning a trespass rather than a crime).

We are looking for a state on Earth in the future where people have more leisure time, where they devote more of their daily lives to an exploration of self – not of ego, but of the soul – in order to understand what they are capable of, to understand that thoughts are living things, that whatever they think is *creation*, and that if they think for the best they will alter the surface and quality of the planet, and the quality of life for everyone else on the planet.

So work needs to change.

As I have said, work wasn't a labour of drudgery in my time, it was a labour of love, and people worked when they felt they could work, and created when they felt they could create. They were encouraged to dream, *to consciously dream*, and we had instruments, we had tools that would focus on creative thought and could solidify, as it were, those thoughts into material objects. We had artists who would think art on to the canvas; we had architects and groups of people who would think buildings into shape.

We had people who would be creative with regard to healing, who would sit in a circle with their patients at its centre, and their image of the patient as being whole would be stronger than the patient's image of their illness. Of course, it was easier for us to heal people then than it is for your doctors and nurses today, because the patient was already of a mind that would accept healing, that would accept the creative power of God within other souls and accept harmony and the involvement of others within their life.

Another aspect of work on the physical plane now is that it very often cuts people off from each other. They have forgotten how to communicate, they have forgotten the niceties of life, they have forgotten to enquire about each other, simply because work is the great 'god'.

And what does it profit them? It brings them motor cars that rust; marriages that don't last; children who never look back at their parents and move on – in a way divorcing themselves from those parents. It brings unrest, it brings anxiety about the new house, or the holiday, or the clothes, or the furnishings, and none of these things are important. It is companionship that is important, the reflection of yourself in others; your uniqueness and the way you share that uniqueness with others. Those are the things that count, those are the things that are important, those are the things that have to be brought back to the surface so that the Earth can be changed.

The second half, the second area I wish to look at this afternoon is THE work...

THE work!

God's work! There was a time not so long ago on Earth when young men and women were called to the priesthood, were 'called' to serve God in this way, or so they thought. They felt they were answering an inner prompting to serve God; but the priesthood is restrictive. Many religious beliefs at the moment are a nonsense, and men and women chain themselves to societies – to organisations – that in truth divorce them from God; that estrange people from God and estrange those who feel they are 'called' from God. Yes, they have a calling, but that calling is not to be a priest within a conventional, mistaken religion. That calling is for them to *develop their spiritual gifts*.

We watch with interest the services that Michael and Jane take, because there is such a mix of people in the congregations. There are people who are afraid of their own spirituality, and those people would make excellent mediums and healers and counsellors. There are people who believe mediumship is theirs to control and to direct and that it must conform to their vision of what they are prepared and not prepared to do, rather than to God's.

There is so much of **THE** work to do, but it requires people to surrender to that call from within, and to say, 'Yes, God, I will do it. Now, what is it I have to do?' Isn't that a leap? 'Yes, God, I will do it.' Full stop. '*Now… what do you want me to do?*' That is what is demanded of the next generation: the faith, the feeling that God has something for them to do, and the courage to answer that feeling by saying, 'I will do it!' Michael's life is an example of this, because his teacher came along at the point where he said, 'Yes, God, I will do it.'

There are many workers – potential workers – out there now. Children who have been born over the past thirty years and those that are being born today have a great potential to transmit and receive spiritual power, communication, information, healing and counselling thoughts. There are many spiritual leaders out there, potentially, but they need to be in the right environment; they need to have parents who understand them; they need to have workmates who will encourage them; they need to be given the freedom of opportunity to grow, not to be tied down to a desk or a production line, but for people to say, 'Here is someone special; we will support that someone special.'

We are about to turn religion on its head. We can't have clergymen growing fat and mediums never being discovered or

175

allowed to work because society says that is the way things should be. We are working towards a society that will recognise the Light-bringers in its midst and support them so that they can do the work they are supposed to do.

Ideally a medium should have no other work except their mediumship. Ideally a medium should be in the company of like-minded people so that his or her talents can be used to the best effect, so that they are always spiritually energised and, at a moment's notice, can help or bring through communication, or can heal, or can speak with the voice of God and of guides.

There has to be a change in thinking. There are little lights out across your world, and those lights are the children who are growing up now and have a mission. And part of what you do, and part of what we want from this book and from your websites, is the opportunity to say to parents whose children have heard and seen 'things', sensed things, children who are 'different' (and most parents know who they are, they will recognise this in their children and many will be afraid of it) that *they have to allow that growth*. They have to be brave enough to know that God wants those children to work, and they have to be brave enough to sacrifice in order that those children can do that work; not to expect them to follow in family tradition or in society's tradition, but to say, 'Here is someone special; we will help them on their way, we will support them in any way we can, so that they can speak with God's voice on behalf of mankind.'

So, my first address today was to say, 'This is what has been wrong; this is why you are as you are at this moment in time.' My second address is to try and point out areas that need to be changed. The work ethic needs to be changed; it is wrong. God does not expect souls to work themselves into an early grave.

That is pointless. There are souls that are born and die that have never appreciated the beauty of a tree; have never cried because of the beauty of a sunset; have never felt the wind touch them; have never breathed clean air; all these gifts the planet has to give they are oblivious to, because all they care about is work, and what is work presently? It is simply a fear of: 'What will I do... how will I make ends meet?'

God provides.

There has to be a pull back from the whole planet revolving around work. There has to be time for souls to contemplate, to meditate, to heal, to give out vibrations of love. They cannot do this if they are working every day and every night at some pointless occupation.

And secondly, for things to change on the Earth the army of Light that is coming has to be *recognised.*

Children who see spirits should not be stifled; parents should not be afraid, they should encourage, they should gather their children together in groups with those who know how to explain what is happening to them. And they should give them the room, the space, to develop as God wants them to develop.

You [*Michael: meaning the three of us*] are here at the beginning of an exciting time for this planet. You will not see it change much physically whilst you are still here in a physical body, but you are here at the beginning. You are pioneers, because the words that are given to you have to be spoken, have to be heard, have to be out there... and there will be a resistance to them. But nothing that is worth doing comes without resistance, and you are, in a way, *revolutionaries* bringing a new way of thinking because God allows us to say these things to you.

In my civilisation, '*Joseph*' (as the equivalent name) meant 'a father'. That was the resonance in that name, and I come to you in the name of *The* Father, and ask The Father to bring you this information. I heard you discussing, over your meal, the fact that in my first address I came through and spoke about the Light energies needed in order to talk to you [*Michael: a reference to a conversation we had had prior to this session*]. It was difficult in the beginning to establish communication with you, but it has become considerably easier, because now you are three. You have three people working for the Light, and there is now energy at your end of the equation that we can work with and can use.

I am surrounded by my brothers and sisters on this side who work with me, and together we will preach the word and get it out to the people. If you want a term for what you are doing, for who you are, you could call yourselves 'The Band of Light'; and perhaps that could go into your books as a term... 'A publication from *The Band of Light*'. Describe yourselves as The Band of Light and, as its symbol, the twin snakes of the healers, of your doctors, of the medical profession – the snakes wound around the central symbol – a derivative of this could be an emblem you carry on your books. This symbol is older than the medical profession knows, and was once applied to knowledge rather than to healing, and represented the taming of the two halves of man's nature, with the sword of truth between the snakes.

I am going to leave you now because Michael is tiring, and I thank you for listening to me, and for chronicling my words, which are the words of many people; not just my words but the words of a vast number of souls from the sphere I reside in. Other personalities will speak to you in future, but I am the spokesperson at this time.

God bless. May you always work in the Light. I will speak to you again very soon.

Chapter Sixteen
Positive and Negative

Joseph: Good morning from my sphere, my area of consciousness. The communication I want to give this morning concerns *positive and negative*.

I'd like to begin with something that you are familiar with, that you play games with – a *domino*, which has white spots on a black background. Were the domino to be white, you would not see the spots and this, in a nutshell, is the nature of positive and negative: one exists to highlight the other. Of course, it is more complicated than that but, at its basic level, one exists to highlight the other. How do you know what you are *not* unless there is something to compare yourself against?

So, to reiterate, this morning I wish to talk about positive and negative – black and white, if you like – and to examine those dual aspects of every person, because in every object, in every soul, in every aspect of creation, there is a positive and a negative side. This causes many problems in your culture because the negative side is not acknowledged, is considered to be something evil and something that should be pushed away from a soul. If you consider most religions, they say that the negative side of a person must be tamed, must be pushed away, and that penance must be done for the acts that are instigated by the dark side of people.

The purpose of a human being is to become *whole*; to balance the positive and the negative. Your religions make a great mistake in identifying anything that is from the negative side as being a *'sin'*. They separate the person rather than bringing the person together, and this is why you have so much trauma and so much violence in your world, because people are fighting *themselves*. In embracing the positive and negative and saying, 'I am both, I am neither,' you get a complete person; but let us go back to the beginning, let us go back to creation and to movement.

In creation you have to have movement, you have to have change, and change is created through *conflict*. I do not mean conflict as in a war or conflict as in fighting between two people but conflict in that there has to be *abrasion*, there has to be one thing rubbing against another. There has to be a friction to create illusion.

The illusion that you are sitting in this morning is based upon friction, is based upon movement. The illusion consists of a construct that is constantly trying to force itself in different directions. The positive side forces in one way, the negative side forces in another, and these two forces that seek dominance between them create an area which is the illusion. That is the nature of creation and this is what people do not understand.

Imagine that the illusion you are in is a sphere. If we have two spheres and one is a black one and the other is a white one, and one has a negative charge and the other a positive charge, they are just two spheres; they are not an illusion, they are not a construct. But when you push them together they try to repel each other, they create movement and an area in which people can dream and construct things.

You have to have *both*; you cannot eradicate the negative from your world. The people whom you describe as 'evil' cannot eradicate the *positive* from your world. You have to have *both* in order for your world to exist. It is *control* over the positive and the negative that the soul is trying to teach itself.

During the Fall – that time many millennia ago when souls lost conscious control of creation – it was the negative side they 'fell' into. The negative side had dominance… not totally, but it was the stronger side – the negative side of dreaming – and so those souls were caught up in violence, they were caught up in aggression, because there was a lack of balance. If the balance between negative and positive is equal, then there is no violence, there is only creation.

I remember that Michael and Jane were taken on a walk and much information was given to them by one of my colleagues on the spirit side as to the nature of negative and positive and I would like to reiterate what was said during that walk [*reference here is being made to an unrecorded communication given to Michael and Jane at a time before they had a digital recorder*].

In each object there has to be a positive and a negative charge. Otherwise, if there were simply a positive charge, that object would last forever. It would never change. It would never crumble. It would never fall apart so that it could be replaced by another object. So, in creation, there is also built into every object a negative charge, and that negative charge, pushing against the positive charge, gives the object the ability to decay.

You look at decay in your world as a terrible thing. Bodies decay; edifices decay; anything that you build eventually decays. Nothing is forever. Your cars are not forever; your televisions are not forever; your houses are not forever. You have to keep the movement going – positive against negative and negative against positive – so that forms can be broken down and recreated as new forms, otherwise you would just have stasis. No one would learn and the illusion would not have the ability to change if there was just stasis.

So all creation, all matter that you perceive, is made up out of a positive and a negative charge. The problem arises when those two charges become out of balance and **what is wrong with your world at the moment is that the negative charge is the dominant one.** It is not in itself corrupt, it is only when mind is put into it, when it is perceived as something that is desirable, that it becomes out of balance. The negative charge takes people towards violence, towards corruption of power, towards wanting to dominate other people. It is the positive side that has become subdued and weaker and what we seek to teach souls is how to build the positive side up again so that there is a balance.

In a way the people that are swept into a wave of evil cannot help themselves because the charge in their body has become negative rather than positive. They still have a positive side but it is subdued. Now, isn't that a different way of looking at mental illness and looking at violence, to say: 'This person is not inherently evil, they have simply succumbed to an excess of negative charge within their psyche' ?

And that, really, is what is happening. It has to do with the echo from 'the Fall'. The Fall occurred within the beginnings – as you would understand it – of creation. It was a time when there were experiments as to how creation could be brought forth. This goes back to my first communication ever with you, when I said that this world was created not by God but by Man or by human souls, and so it was, and also the physical universe to some extent. That is not to say that God is not present in everything – He is – but He gave His Children charge over their realm.

...He gave His Children charge over their realm and on Earth *they got it wrong*.

There was an imbalance, there was an overwhelming ego with some souls and they said: 'I deserve more than you. I am intellectually more powerful than you and I am creatively more powerful than you. I will look after the rest of you (because at that stage they were saying this with good intention) but I think that you should look to me because I am of a greater spirituality than you, I have a greater insight than you' ...and at that point they began to corrupt the Eden that was originally created on Earth. As they began to draw more upon the negative side their initial desire to do good for others – albeit from an egoistic point of view – also became corrupted and became more violent, and they forgot who they were.

They forgot who they were!

And this predominance of the negative state swept across all souls so that, whether they had been builders or destroyers, they became charged negatively. What we are seeking to do from the spirit side is to lift souls up from that negative viewpoint to a point where, through what we say to them and through the way that they look at this world and each other through teaching, the positive side becomes more dominant. Not supremely dominant, because then you would have stagnation, you would not have evolution, and the point of this illusion is also to evolve. *As above, so below*. The illusion is supposed to change, supposed to evolve, supposed to become more God-like, so that within the illusion we discover more about the nature of God.

We have to build people's positive sides up and we do not do that through condemnation, we do that by example and by saying: 'What if you thought in this way? What if we gave you a series of instructions you could follow and prove for yourself that they work – that would be a benefit to yourself and also to mankind?' and to prove to people, step by step, that there is another way to think. Then we build up the white side – the White Light – and we expel some of the darkness and balance comes back into play.

Positive and negative, of course, begin in a thought state within each soul... You have certain souls who jump out of bed in a morning and say, 'This is going to be a wonderful day,' and for them it *is* a wonderful day. You have souls who stay in bed and shut the curtains and say, 'This is going to be another terrible day,' and it *is* another terrible day because they are giving each day a spin or a charge mentally. They give their bodies a spin or a charge mentally. You have souls who say, 'I feel well today! Aren't I well today!' and they *are*; then you have souls who say, 'I am miserable today! I am ill today! I am filled with aches and pains today!' and they *are*. **So there is a physical charge that follows on from the mental charge.**

But there is also a spiritual charge... The souls who believe that they are in the darkness in the illusion and are not worthy of God's Love create that unworthiness of God's Love and create a barrier between themselves and the Light. The souls who say, 'Today we are God's angels; today we can make a difference; today we can bring the Light to people' do so because they put a positive spin into their souls.

Souls are learning to create on all levels. They create first on the Earth plane then, when they move away, onwards and upwards from the Earth plane, they continue to create. They create with more instant results because anything that they think of can instantly be seen around them. And as they progress further up the spiritual ladder, as it were, they create their environments (they actually do on a lower level but they are not as aware of it). There comes a time where they create their own entire universe using positive and negative charges. I do so... I have my own 'world.' You may think it strange for each soul to have a world but you have houses... and aren't those houses *your own little world*? Are you not encased within a world of your own thoughts, even at this stage?

It is simply that, as you grow more God-like, you are able to project and mould those thoughts more effectively than you do on Earth. The dominant vibration on Earth is, of course, negative – so you are constantly combating, whenever you make an approach towards another person or step out of your front door into the illusion, you are constantly combating the negativity of millions of minds.

Spiritual evolution takes longer than it should do; people should not have to reincarnate and reincarnate (which, of course, as you know, is their wish). *They shouldn't have to do it.* Within two or three lifetimes they should be learning and appreciating their creative ability and saying, 'Now it is time for me to move on, there are more exciting adventures for me!' but instead they are pulled back by the negativity of this plane.

And when they die, when they pass over, their desire is once again to be immersed in the negativity with all its pain and suffering. That might sound strange but that is the dominant vibration in their soul when they pass over and so they are not interested in the Light. I hope that explains why so many souls want to come back; they are presented with dazzling landscapes, with beautiful souls in front of them, with the ability to move onwards and upwards into glory and into Light, but instead they choose to come back to a very dark Earth because they are comfortable with it, because they are used to it, and because it is the dominant vibration surrounding their souls.

God wishes every soul to be like Him. Every soul is a part of Him but God forces out His Children into the darkness and says: 'Learn. Come back to Me as a God yourself, come back to Me just like Me and then all of us can evolve to a greater plane.' There are greater planes yet that God can inhabit, so God *is evolving*. Why should God be static? God is a mixture of positive and negative fields of energy, so God, too, seeks to evolve, to become more.

As above, so below – each of you is seeking to become more than you were when you incarnated. God seeks to become more, to expand, and God expands by the experiences of His Children being brought back to Him. If those experiences are negative then the soul cannot reach Him. God says: 'Go out and learn, go out and see how to create, how to care for people, how to care for your own children that one day you will send forth into the ether to learn.' It is an ongoing, growing process, but in this little backwater it is a slow process because there is this immersion in the misdeeds of the past, in the mistaken thinking of the past, that overhangs into the present.

What a wonderful potential you have for healing souls – and I am not talking about souls that are ill (although they require healing), I am talking about souls who have embraced, as it were, the dark side of things, the negative side of things. This is why we ask you to send out the Light because, in sending out the Light, you are boosting the positive side of a soul's psyche.

If a soul is lying in a hospital bed believing that it is dying from a dreadful disease – that is a negative charge. So you have to send out Light to that soul, you have to embrace that soul in Light, so that the positive side can be given more prominence. That is how you get wellbeing; wellbeing is simply *balance* and I hope that now makes sense as to why we often say in churches: 'Send out the Light to people, surround them with Light.' That is the most effective healing you can send to them; send out Light to the cells because within each cell there is a positive and a negative side; send out Light into their lives so that they can see life in a more balanced way.

The most effective thing you can do for anyone is to send out Light to them because the White Light is the positive side of creation.

The negative side is not evil; on a cosmic or God-level the negative charge is not evil; it is necessary for substance. God is not evil, God is Love and God has negative and positive contained within Him. They are not Him, they are His *tools*. It is the same for His Children; the negative and the positive charges are the tools of souls who at the moment are entombed within negative lives on Earth. It is like them being given this wonderful tool chest and burying it in the ground; they do not understand that they can use negative and positive to create.

189

If you paint a picture you are using negative and positive energies; your creativity puts Light into the painting but, because positive cannot exist without negative, inherent in every brush stroke there is also the means of that painting's eventual destruction. Not because that is an evil thing but because it will at some stage in its existence have to give way to something else – hopefully a better expression of the painting.

Every thought that you have is negative and positive; every thought that you send out – even your thoughts of healing – are not totally positive. You cannot have a totally positive thought. You have to have a thought that is a balance of negative and positive. *That* is the thought that does no harm – the thought that is balanced.

Can you then see the destructive power of negative thoughts, when people actually will other people to death? When people actually hate those who have transgressed against them? They send out thoughts that are negatively charged and those thoughts attach themselves to the negative charge of the soul that they are directed towards, emphasising the negative side and causing chaos.

Too much of the negative side and you have chaos, too much of the positive side and you have stasis. **Chaos and stasis moving together are creation.**

Your religions say: 'We will cast out the Evil One. You must cast out the Evil One, the sin from yourself'. In embracing the negative side of yourself you become a whole person, you become in control of that negative side. By trying to push it away it becomes a thing to be feared and fear is a negative emotion, so you are adding to the negative side.

You are told by certain of your religions that you must never have base thoughts, never have violent thoughts. The key is not to not have those thoughts but not to take notice of them, not to give them a charge. You are in a Field of thoughts and so, as receptors, as souls, there will of course be access to violent thoughts at times, to sexual thoughts at times that are off-key, to thoughts against other people that are not born of love.

And what does religion teach you to do about these things? It teaches you to push them away, but in pushing them away *you give them power*. In pushing them away they become stronger and begin to dominate your life. Whereas, were you to see them as simply something that was floating through your consciousness, something you are simply observing that is nothing to do with you, you would not give them a negative or a positive charge and they would have no power over you. This is why meditation is so important; in meditation you see your thoughts and you see the thoughts that come through your mind that are not your own but exist within the sphere that you are living in.

Many religions teach you to feel guilty; teach you to feel bad. Why, when you are supposed to be a blend of the positive and the negative, should you feel bad about your negative side? In embracing and loving your negative side it doesn't have the power for perversion that it has if you try and push it away.

If you try to embrace your positive side too aggressively you become like many religious representatives that are static beings, unable to think outside the envelope they have created and placed themselves in. They start out with good intentions but they are unable to see beyond that positivity. They become static. You have to have the blend to be a rounded soul.

I am a blend of positive and negative energies. I control the positive and negative energies; I have controlled them in order to speak to you this morning. I do not consider myself to be an evil being, neither do I consider myself to be a good being. I am a traveller who has certain tools at his disposal that will allow me to progress and to become more God-like.

If I give you a piece of paper, if I put it in front of you, is that piece of paper positive or negative? You decide! The moment that you decide it becomes positive or negative within the field of your own mind. And we say to you, 'Pray for people who do damage to you, pray for your enemy' because they *become more of your enemy* if you think of them negatively.

Every object in this room has within it positive and negative fields but it is your mind that instructs each object as to what it shall be within your mental field. So you can have a house that you hate and that hates you back. You can have a house that you love and that loves you back. You can have a house that is neutral, with you putting love or negative feelings into it as you feel you should do. Each object responds to you; it is only neutral when it is not involved in your mental field.

What you should do with each object is to approach it *from the heart*. In the heart the thoughts that come to you are already blended because they are God-thoughts; they are already a mixture and a balance of positive and negative. The thoughts that come from the mind, which can only relate to the physical Field around it, are corrupt almost from the time of your birth because they are infused with the mental Field of the illusion that you are passing through.

Thinking from the heart-mind is so important for the creation of a new vista to place in front of souls and around them. The thoughts that come to you from your heart via your soul (which exists on a higher level than this – remember that your soul is not actually here, it is existing at a higher level, it is linked to God) – the thoughts that come from your soul are balanced.

So, if something disturbs you, embrace it in love from the heart-mind and you will balance the charge within it. If a person disturbs you, surround them with love from the heart-mind and they will be powerless because the balance from the heart-mind, the natural state of things, is balance. If you project balance to someone then you overcome their own charge eventually, if enough of you do it. And there will be a time on your Earth when people will sit in great buildings and will send out balanced love to people, love from the heart-mind.

If you send out love to someone from your mind it already has a bias, it already has a charge, even in the most balanced of you, because you send out love *conditionally*: 'I will love you because I want you to change'. No! 'I will love you because it is my duty to do so in a balanced way. What you do with that love is up to you.'

People will sit in great buildings to send out love to the world and then we are 'going places', then we are truly changing things!

Have you any questions on this subject?

Jane: Before the Fall, what was the purpose of the Earth, what was the balance? What were we supposed to do with the positive and negative?

Joseph: If you on Earth are going to a cinema, you enjoy the entertainment for a while; you may identify with the actors in the film... or you may watch a play and the play unfolds around you and you are lost in that excitement, that enjoyment. A soul cannot be static. **God's Children exist to experience.** They exist through experience and experience is limitless, experience goes on forever and ever and ever. Amen.

The original intention of this sphere, this area of space, was to give the soul experience; not to have the abomination of violence, but to give the soul a condition to experience itself in.

The soul, as I said at the beginning, is composed of a negative and a positive charge at soul level. It has to have that movement of the two in order to experience itself, otherwise it would still exist but would not be aware, would not be aware of movement and of change and the soul seeks *experience*. This is the reason why God sent his Children forward, because God wished to experience.

Look at your Bible – '*In the beginning there was The Word.*' '*Let there be Light!*'... Light in the darkness – that was the beginning of the shift that created this plane. Light in the darkness, Light against the darkness, that created the illusion. And into this world then came those souls who wished to experience what this particular illusion had to offer.

There are other vibrations, other subtleties of lightness and darkness that create other illusions for the soul to go through. It is amazing that souls wish to come back time and again to this little sphere of influence when there are other illusions they can be born into; other realities that can give them other challenges. But it is all a film, it is all a play. It exists to help the soul evolve but it is an illusion.

So, before the Fall there was a balance and the balance existed as a playground. You have images of Utopia, you have images of Eden, you have images from your Bible of Paradise, and that is what the sphere was like. The sphere was balanced because the Earth was an equal mixture of positive and negative.

The Earth at the moment is corrupted by the dominant, negative thoughts of the souls that live on it, and reacts (as it is supposed to) against that and creates chaos within itself. It wasn't always like that – once the Earth was balanced. The Earth was a different colour from the Earth that you now see; the Earth was predominantly green and silver when viewed from space and was at a different angle. The angle of the Earth has shifted because of the successive generations of negativity that have been fed into it. There have been cataclysms that have wiped out civilisations and they came from this imbalance.

We are not talking in terms of a few years here; we are talking about a planet that has been around for millennia and has been populated by souls *before*. And then came the mistaken way of thinking, way of dreaming, that caused the cut-off from God (in thought only – no one is ever cut off from God completely), and what we are bringing is a rediscovery of the God-within. It is as simple as that. God does not cut off His Children; His Children cut themselves off from God. It is a simple matter of thinking, of re-balancing thought, that enables those souls to reconnect with God and to bring through that paradise that was lost – *Paradise Lost* – and the paradise will first be brought through in the way that people think and then will begin to manifest itself outside of themselves in the Field that they have created en masse.

If you are asking whether angels were involved in the Fall, unfortunately, yes, they were, because they were the first-born of God, and to describe yourselves as *fallen angels* would, in some part, be correct. Michael has long-believed that angels never incarnate in human form. Well, no, they don't, not at present, but *they did* and the human soul and the angelic soul are only separated by a tiniest degree of the ethereal.

God's first-choice for His Children was to create the angels. If you were to look at an angelic body that was subjected to the corruption of the negative Field that was immersed in the illusion of the negative Field for millennia, then you would not see the great beings that Michael sometimes sees and talks to. You would see something very like a human being. The two paths lead back to God, and the two paths lead to a merging, but not all of the angels were involved in the Fall.

I feel it is time to leave Michael, unless there are any further questions?

Jane: I am not sure about this ...but isn't suffering a means of people expressing love to other people? If everyone was alright, how would love be expressed between people? So, before the Fall were there other difficulties and sufferings, or was everyone just 'happy'?

Joseph: Madam, I have to say that that is an outrageous, *outrageous* way of looking at God's Love!

If you have a guinea pig, or a cat, or a rabbit, does that pet have to suffer before you can love it? Love is a self-sustaining state of being. Bliss creates bliss and it is never God's wish for anyone and it is never *our* wish for anyone to suffer. Suffering is loss of connection with God, it is loss of that 'radio-signal' that connects you to 'Radio-God'! It is perpetuation of the negative field that feeds itself that creates suffering.

These changes took place over many, many years and the Field was imbalanced over many, many years as you would understand it. The suffering that exists in your sphere is entirely the soul's own responsibility and entirely the result of a history of too much negativity.

It is nothing to do with God... God as *All* exists as Love and wishes His Children to experience that limitless, that endless Love. And you love each other because you are part of that field of Love, not because there is a lack you feel that in superiority you can fulfil. That is a perversion of Love. We do not love because people are suffering, we love because we *can*; we love because we *must*, we love because *we are Love*. Anything else is an imbalance of the negative and positive fields.

You should not love to alleviate suffering; you should love because it is your natural state and then, when it is everyone's natural state to love, suffering will not be there. You create the balance again. You do not attack the suffering with love, you re-establish the soul-identity of the person you are sending love to with love. Then that soul withdraws itself from the suffering and realises that the suffering is something they have bought into.

Every soul that suffers is suffering because they have bought into that suffering; and they have bought into that suffering to a greater or lesser degree because of their belief or reliance on the negative Field.

Is it not true that your society is based on the negative? Not on balance, but on the negative? You are told from the minute you can understand that you are growing old, that you are growing sick, that you are dependent, that you are going to die,

197

that you have needs – you need money, you need food, you need clothes, you are dependent upon each other...

You are dependent only on God! In the amount or degree that you love God, so your world creates wealth and riches around you. Do you seriously think that, at the end of the week, your boss is the person that is responsible for giving you your living? Your living, your maintenance, your being comes from God.

Did you require money as a part of God? Did you have a care as part of God? It is only when you come here and become entrenched in the negative Field that you buy into the Field's perpetuating need. The Field seeks to control you because the Field is a thought; it is a thought that is fed by many thoughts. The Field is very comfortable with being more negative than positive because it is fed.

What you must seek to do is to love that Field into balance; not into non-existence, but into balance. Then you will see emerging the Utopia you have been told about through so many civilisations, going back as far as the human race can remember.

You love because you are Love, not because you can give it.

I am going to withdraw from the instrument now. I am satisfied with the communication and I will speak with you a little later today [*a reference to Joseph's introduction and conclusion to Revelation, which were given later on the day of this communication*].

Chapter Seventeen
Power

Michael's observations: During the concluding session for this book Joseph talks with obvious sadness about the illusion of earthly power and gives more details of the Fall and its consequences before changing pace and painting at some length an enthralling picture of the idyllic nature and structure of the society he was once a part of. For us this chapter and Joseph's afterword simultaneously represented the completion of *Revelation* and the beginning of *Illumination*, Joseph's second book, which he would segue into almost immediately, leaving us with little time to catch our collective breaths, such was his urgency in delivering his communications to the world! Little did I realise when Joan's comments prompted the delivery of the title you are holding (see introduction), that Joseph had an agenda of communication that has, at the time of writing this updated introduction to this section, filled five volumes with a sixth in preparation...

Michael: I can see Joseph. He hasn't moved in close yet. He seems to be attempting to overshadow me...

'Good day,' he says.

He has brought with him some branches from the sphere in which he lives, which are scented, and which he says he has brought literally to clear the air. [*Michael: Joseph overshadows me at this point.*]

Joseph: It is so important in all spiritual work that the cleansing ritual takes place before any communication takes place, because, as human beings, you pick up so very much from the atmosphere that surrounds you – so much pollution. Often it is difficult for us to link with you because of the amount of negative vibration that is within your auras; and this is just from ordinary things; this is not as a result of great challenges in life, or trauma or illness or violence. These are just the everyday, drifting vibrations that are in your atmosphere, that are in your minds, in your houses; and so I have brought these branches to melt into the atmosphere and to cleanse it.

I wish to tell you that lime, the fruit and the essence of the lime, are very good for cutting vibrations; it is the colour of the fruit and the particular vibration of its essence that are useful in cleansing. We used to use lime to treat illness as part of the cleansing ritual. We would wash our patients with a solution of lime juice and water, because this took away not only any oils on the body – anything that would hold negative vibrations – but also took away anything that was clinging to the illness from 'outside'. Anything that was contributing to their illness would be taken away temporarily by the use of lime juice.

I am now attempting to move further in towards Michael, who has a full stomach [*Michael*: *we were sitting just after lunch!*] and that is not a good idea if I am to talk to you, but, nevertheless, I am attempting to do so. I want to speak this afternoon, as I have said, about power and the way in which humans perceive power.

From the time that the current race is born to the time that it goes to the grave, it concerns itself with the acquisition of power. You can see it in children – in siblings – you can see how there is always a dominant sibling. You can see it in animals, as there is always a dominant animal in a pack. And then, as life progresses, as souls grow physically, power becomes more and more important to the ego.

Power is seen as a means of attaining immortality, and so it is sought on every level. It is not just your politicians who thirst for power, the thirst goes from the highest to the lowest, right down to the person who, at any gathering, will attempt to dominate that gathering so that he or she feels powerful. In the workplace, too, there are always people who seek to be ahead of the others because they lust for power. Even when there is no structured power base they will assume one – create one – so that they can say, 'I am more powerful than you are.'

This lust for power lies deep within the soul of every human being. It was the original problem – the original sin, if you like, in that the Ancient Ones, the ones who 'fell', wanted power. They had power beyond measure when compared against the present human being; but they wanted more and more and they wanted it for themselves, to feel that it originated from themselves.

Their mistake was:

(1) The misuse of that power, and

(2) Believing that they were worthy of it and that they could create it themselves. Of course, and this is the entire point of this lecture, all power comes from *One Source*.

All power comes from God, and God-power is unpolluted, God-power is pure because it doesn't judge. God does not seek to manipulate His Children. God does not seek to segregate His Children. God does not give out power or energy because He wants something back; He simply exists to give out power to the souls that have journeyed out from His Centre. And there the mistake was made at the time of the Fall. It is the 'original sin': to question God's abilities and motives. To say: 'Why should God have all of the power, when I can have some? When, in certain areas, I know better than God?'

Such arrogance!

And that is the second original sin – to say, 'I know better than God...'

Do you?

If you have no power except that which comes from God, how can you second-guess what God's intentions are?

God's intentions are always pure, are always loving.

The third original sin was to look at the Earth as it was then and believe that things were wrong with it, that it could be improved upon, and to say, 'God is not putting them right... but I/we can...'

Can you?

Did they?

No. They, as we said earlier, became lost in their own dream of power. The power was an illusion. They built a dream and immersed themselves in it, and so became 'separated', through their own choice and their own free will, from the God that still loved them, despite what they had done.

They banished themselves. This is where *the Fall* I am talking about differs from the Fall of biblical legend. God banished no one; they banished themselves and were lost in the darkness.

At that point, the shift – the emphasis – because these souls were powerful on Earth with corrupted energy, changed. At that point was born a struggle for earthly power. And that struggle, the effects of which can still be seen today, was evident at first in a change to the animal kingdoms, with one animal killing another animal not just to survive but also to take from the other the power it believed the other animal contained.

The emphasis, the shift, in thinking was towards there being a need for power in order to survive. And souls have to re-learn now, in this age, that they need nothing but God in order to survive, *nothing but God*. You can still see the echoes in your world of what went wrong, and you can see that the lesson is being taught repeatedly without being learned:

Power – or the illusion of power – corrupts.

Every soul initially yearns for power for the right reasons, and is really expressing its desire to change things for the better for all, thinking, 'If I come to power, then things will be different.'

But because the power it seeks is not the power of God, but the illusion of power that goes back to the time of the Fall, they buy into that echo, they buy into that earthly vibration, which is corrupt. Very few souls are strong enough to wield earthly power without it corrupting them.

There has to be a shift in the way that people perceive power. First of all they have to understand that power on Earth does not exist as anything other than a corrupted and spiritually impotent vibration. Power on Earth, since the time of the Fall, has never been used for good. In many companies it is not used for good. In politics it is not used for good. You see its misuse in domestic situations as well, where one partner seeks power over the other. It is never used for good.

The simplest way to draw the correct power into your soul is to say, 'I am nothing. I know nothing. God has a plan for me. Father I am open to that energy.'

People, souls, should be sitting today in your world not just to meditate and to discover who they really are, spiritually, but to say, 'God, I am sitting today in order that your power can flow through me.' That power would then allow them to heal; that power would allow them to talk to other dimensions as you are doing now. That power would allow them to see through the corruption of religion. I find it amusing that today there has been talk on this subject and that souls buy so resolutely into the 'ideal' of religion, which is itself linked into that original sin [*Michael: again, Joseph had been listening to our conversations.*]

Your religions are about power, not about God. People attend churches blindly, Sunday after Sunday, to worship not God, but the ministers; to worship the power they feel the ministers have, when they should be sitting quietly in their homes, with their families around them, going within themselves and praying thus: 'God give me the power to do whatever you want me to do. Give me the power to be without ego so that I can help people. Give me the power to see through the illusion so that I am not chasing for half my life or more something that cannot be chased, so that I am not basing a whole incarnation on something that is unobtainable.'

I am not saying that you should not work. There is pleasure in the construction of ideas and the construction of physical things, but work should not be based upon the acquisition of power. I am not saying that you should not hold political views, but your political views should be based upon what the soul, the heart, says to you; what you believe morally about people, situations, lands and the Earth, not upon the colour of a flag and on whether you will pay less taxes.

All men are equal; they are created equal. Their journey back home to God is at differing rates, but they are equal. No one is above anyone else. Has this not been said to you since the beginning of time? And yet some souls feel they are better than other souls, that they know better than other souls as to what those other souls should be doing; and always there is this seeking of power. 'When I come to power I will change the world!'

No.

You won't.

You will change the world only if God wishes you to change the world, and you can only know if that is what He wishes you to do if you tune into God-power.

When I was on Earth we used God-power to literally move mountains. Do you believe that a chasm could be filled in by God-power?

...Of course it can.

Do you think that an area of mountainous region or tundra could be changed so that we could grow crops? We changed it by praying, we changed it by visualising the change; we changed it by bringing through God-power; and before we altered anything natural we prayed that it was God's will that it be thus changed, and that, if we made a mistake along the way, we could re-establish the order of things in accordance with God's natural laws. We always checked ourselves, and we gathered together, sometimes in our thousands, to pray in order to change things, and that is how we moved mountains.

We eliminated many diseases that you now suffer from again, because we chased them out by using God-power and by saying, 'You have no power over us, you are an illusion.'

If we had citizens – souls – with minds that were unbalanced or unstable, we would sit with them; we would see them as whole again; we would literally *change their minds* by the power of the God-within we were drawing on, always knowing that we didn't make the change, but that God did.

And then came the Fall and everything changed. And things on Earth are not progressing as quickly as they should in the scheme of things, in God's plan, because man is once again investing in the illusion of power.

It is a concept I have been trying to get across to Michael for a couple of weeks because it is one that is close to my heart. You may say that I use power to communicate with you. I do, but it is God-power. It is by God's will that I speak to you today. It is only by God's will that I exist, that you exist, that this communication is possible. *God's will.*

And God's will is that you should have better lives than you are having in order to live closer to Him, in order to realise who you are. You do not do this by chasing rainbows. You do this by communicating with the God-within.

That talent, that ability to move mountains, is still with you, because you are still God's Children, as you were at the time of the Fall. You still have that ability, but you do not use it.

There is too much mammon. There is too much illusion in front of you, too much technology, too much glitter, too much glamour and not enough God-substance. But if enough of you joined together, you would then see what God is capable of through man. And that time has to come, that is what we are working towards.

We would ask those of you who read this to pray to God that, if it is His will, you gravitate towards like-minded people, those you can sit with, those you can work with, those you can contact on the telephone half a world away and say, 'Sit with me, join with me,' so that a nucleus forms; a core of people using God-power.

This is a revolution, but it is not a revolution about earthly power, it is a bloodless revolution. It is a revolution that changes men's minds. You need enough people to do this; enough people who will agree that they will tune in to God, and will agree to do God's will in conjunction with others. 'I will change this

Earth into a new Eden, and I will work to realise it, even though I will not see it in my generation.'

You have no idea of the powerful being each of you is. This forgetfulness of who you are was caused by the Fall and its vibrations still reach out even now, even though they are weaker than they were.

If only you knew the things you are capable of! You, YOU, a single soul, can move mountains if only you believe. Did the Christ not say it?

But you do not believe...

I shall talk to you for a little while about Atlantis because I know that it fascinates you:

There was an abundance of water around our peninsular. There was a coast on three sides; eventually on four sides, but initially on three. Water was used as a sacred element and to power many of the devices we had in our houses.

We used steam, we used water pressure, and, of course, in using water there was no pollution and we could recycle exactly what we had put into our houses and our council chambers. And we always thanked the spirit within for allowing us to have this element, which was precious to us, around us.

We worked metal. We worked gold, but by a different principle than you use today. It did not involve heat in the way that you understand it. It involved the manipulation of the molecules within the metal to reorganise them into the desired shape. We had devices that would do this, and they were based upon principles we understood but which you have lost completely. The energies involved were clean; they did not pollute.

We had ways of bending and shaping metal that would allow us to make quite large structures, and many of our buildings were built out of metal rather than of stone.

We were seafarers and we took to other lands something of – but not all of – our technology. We taught in the area of the world that today is home to the Arabic nations, and it disturbs us to see that there is upset at the moment within what was once one of the planet's most advanced and peaceful cultures.

We took artefacts to the region that today is Egypt, which in itself was far more advanced than your historians realise, and we traded in energy at one stage. We had vessels that would hold Light and hold Light-power; nothing to do with electricity but everything to do with spirit power, and we took these to far lands.

We enjoyed luxury in our lives but we always realised that the luxury came from God; that it was on loan to us. We saw nothing wrong with being rich, with being jewelled and having the good things of the Earth around us, because we knew that these things came from God, and if God wanted us to be this way then that is the way we should be.

The only reason that there is poverty now on the Earth is because – again, harking back to the vibrations of the Fall – your religions have bought into and used as a tool, used as a crowbar, the concept that being poor is noble. It is not noble; it is an affront to God. You are saying to God, 'You give me all these riches but I know you want me to be poor. You are rich but I am not worthy to be rich.' How can you not be worthy to be rich when you are a part of God? *You share in the Kingdom.*

This is what we want the older souls to remember, those that are trapped on the Earth in a constant cycle of reincarnation; those who prefer to be on Earth. We are trying to say to them, 'You share in the Kingdom. You are Children of God. Welcome home.' And at the point that they hear and believe us they will awaken and things will change.

Your technology and your buildings are vastly different than ours. They seem to us cold and brutal. Ours were warm and organic; ours welcomed people and we built small. Yes, we had imposing buildings, but we built small. We didn't crowd the skies; we didn't build close to other buildings.

We had street-lamps that were lit by the same endless energy source, so our roads were lighted.

And, yes, we could travel in the air too, but this secret was kept from other nations. It was the same power used to power our machines, which did not have moving parts, and our lanterns, that we put into our Light vessels. They were guided and directed by thought and by energy. Everything was simple; everything was based upon God-power.

We had a council. Its members were constantly vetted for their intentions. There were many women on that council, as there was an equality between the sexes; we saw no difference between the sexes. We had what you would call sub-committees; we had people who represented areas of land and townships, and always their voices would be heard.

We held great festivals of Light, and I mean *festivals of Light*, of which your fireworks – invented by the Chinese – are another echo. We used Light to light up the skies, but it was Light that was an application of God-energy with a concentration of colours and textures within the fabric of the clouds themselves. This Light had nothing to do with gunpowder; it was not violent.

Our festivals were based upon respect for each other. There was not debauchery in our time. There was very little crime apart from that caused by those who were mentally disturbed. We did not treat people who had transgressed against us in the way that you do; we did not lock them up. We placed them with families who would love them. We surrounded them with so much love that they could not help but let go of the ways of thought that had made them violent or had made them do something criminal in the first place. They had to let things go.

So we were an ordered, loving society and we were long-lived. You will be shocked to hear that the average lifespan on Earth of a typical Atlantean was close to two hundred and eighty years. You have so many pollutants; pollutants of the mind and of the body and soul now, that your corporeal existence is a short one compared to ours.

You do not believe that you can live longer, you do not believe that you are a part of God, you do not believe in the Light, and so the Light goes out in your physical bodies so much more quickly than it did in ours.

Our funerals were celebrations because most of us were psychic enough to still sense the presence of the people who had left; to be able to see them still. And, yes, we mourned the physical presence, but there was also a celebration that the person had gone on ahead to prepare somewhere for us, to prepare for our passage over.

We were given an indication of when we were to pass, to die, so not one of us died without *knowing* that we were going to die, so that we could prepare, so that we could withdraw from this world for a time and finish up our affairs before we went. And there were few accidents because we didn't have the heavy technology that you have.

Our weather was controlled, was clement, because we did not disturb the natural forces, so we didn't have floods, we didn't have tempests or volcanoes erupting until the Fall, which changed everything.

We kept animals, and some of us ate meat, but most were vegetarian. We had animals you don't have now on Earth. We had an animal that you might call the origin of the domestic cow, but with far longer hair or fur than a cow has now, and with horns. We kept what you would consider to be exotic animals indoors, and we kept birds of paradise, parakeets and parrots in our houses, and they had nothing to fear from us.

Many of our houses were open to the skies and to the sun, apart from particular chapels that we chose to close off from the connection with the Earth on all sides, so that within them, in the inner silence, we could commune with God.

We had great libraries, we had great learning, and most people were educated enough to take part in and appreciate that learning. We were overjoyed with people's spoken opinion of things. Even if we didn't agree with their views we felt that they added to the mix and so no one was 'beaten down' because they voiced a difference of opinion from the mainstream.

It sounds like Utopia and it was. It was a paradise on Earth; and Earth was designed to be a paradise, where the human condition could express its joy at being a part of God, and celebrate its separation from God and its oneness with God and itself at the same time, not in pain, but in surroundings that were glorious and which glorified God.

Our mission as a society, as we saw it, was to go out and share our secrets with the other nations of the world. It wasn't just Atlantis that was great; The area that today is Egypt had great powers and great secrets. You look at the pyramids and guess completely wrongly about them and their purpose today. In the area of Syria there was great computing power or the equivalent of it. And life was a wonderful celebration of meeting with new nations and new souls. You greeted everyone as a brother or a sister, because you knew that here you had met up with another element of yourself, and this was a cause for celebration.

I am telling you all this not to pull down your spirits, but to say that things can be so again, will be so again, *have to be so again*; but first there has to be great change.

Change comes not through complex mechanisms but through simple ones, and change begins by saying, 'God, here am I. Make me a light. Give me your power. Let me remember that, with or without your power, I am nothing except a part of You, in which case I am Everything. Show me what to do. Show me where to go.' Then the Light goes out into the world through you and the world changes.

I am growing tired. The Earth plane is a plane of sadness for me. It saddens me that the apple has become rotten, where once there was such beautiful-tasting fruit. But such is the nature of

God that everything that is damaged, everything that is polluted, can once again be glorified; and I must leave you with that thought until our next meeting.

An Afterword by Joseph

I would like to conclude this volume by praying that you have absorbed from it what you, as an individual soul, need to absorb; that you have found it challenging and thought-provoking; that it has smashed a hole in your world through which, and into which, the Light can shine.

Life should never be the same again for you and you will have a thousand questions. I will arrange, through the group that works with me, to answer as many of them as I am able to in future volumes.

My love goes to each of you – it is true love.

I wish nothing from you.

If you love me, I love you in return.

If you hate me, I love you in return.

Each of you reading this volume is my true brother, is my true sister. You are part of my family. I am distanced from you only by vibration but I will be aware of and I will be in touch with each of you who reads this book because the book is composed of my thoughts and when you begin to read it we will be connected for a short time and I will bless each of you who does so.

So, for now, farewell, and my thanks go those who have tirelessly worked to place this volume before you. They have done this because, like me, they are concerned about you, because they wish to suggest that there is a different way for you to look at life, to suggest that there are things you can do to take control of your life, to suggest that there are things you can do to better the lives of others.

And is that such a bad thing?

Also available in **The Joseph Communications** series:

Illumination
change yourself, change the world
...A powerful spiritual manual for personal and global transformation.

Time is running out – Earth is heading for cataclysm. This vitally important book reveals how each of us can literally save the world ...before it's too late.

We need to change and accept personal responsibility now – or Joseph warns there are only three generations left. The Field has become so polluted by mankind's negative energy that the planet cannot sustain itself much longer ...unless radical changes are made to the way we think.

It is our responsibility to renew the Field by infusing it with sufficient Light to redress the balance and return the planet to the paradise it originally was. Illumination provides all the 'tools' to achieve personal and global enlightenment empowering the reader to direct Light and transmute our negativity into harmony, joy, love, peace and spiritual progression.

There is a great urgency to Joseph's words - we do not have an infinite number of tomorrows in which to put things right.

'Read the book, adopt its practices and discover a new life of spiritual harmony and lasting fulfilment.' Jan Quigley.

'A masterpiece of spiritual work! What is very clever is the way Joseph builds up his case throughout this book with possibilities to test his meditations as you go – this is not dry theory! I will certainly continue the daily Light-work which I now regard as essential.' Tony Cross.

'If you wish to bring peace, joy and abundance to yourself and those you love then this book gives you means.' Mr. C. Fraser-Malcolm (Amazon)

'Joseph's chapter on religion couldn't have been closer to my own thoughts!' Liz House.

ISBN: 978-1-906625-09-2

Available from good bookshops, Amazon or direct from thejosephcommunications.us

Also available as an e-Book and audiobook.

Also available in **The Joseph Communications** series:

Your Life After Death
...your final destination is anything but final!

Countless opportunities and wonders wait for you beyond physical death.

Authored by Joseph, a highly evolved spirit who has lived in an enlightened sphere of reality 'beyond the veil' for thousands of years, this new book delivers arguably the most comprehensive account ever written of what lies ahead for you when you leave this world behind.

An essential source of comfort and inspiration, Your Life After Death is the definitive guide to the afterlife...

... read it and you'll never look at the next life, or, indeed, this one, in quite the same way again.

'Packed with very important information, which should have been made available many, many years ago.'
David Feuerstein.

'The book is outstanding and one of immense value to humanity particularly in contrast to the mumbo-jumbo we are exposed to in various religions and philosophies.'
Scott Rabalais.

'Over the years I have read many books on this subject but none have been more informative and in-depth.'
Peggy Sivyer.

'I have never sat up nearly all night and read a book from cover to cover in one go before and it has had a major impact on me.'
Valerie Ann Riddell.

'The beautiful journey of on-going evolution for the soul described in the book is profoundly meaningful and "feels" so right.'
Eugenie Heraty.

ISBN: 978-1-906625-03-0

Available from good bookshops, Amazon or direct from thejosephcommunications.us
Also available as an e-Book and audiobook.

Also available in **The Joseph Communications** series:
the Fall
you were there, it's why you're here
...aeons ago everything changed.
AND YOU WERE THERE!
There is so much more to you than you imagine.

You have forgotten the cataclysm that created today's dysfunctional societies and wounded planet...

In **the Fall**, Joseph seeks to reactivate that astonishing inner knowledge of your spiritual origins.

Each chapter is a eureka moment and, by the last page, many, if not *all*, of those elusive answers regarding existence and the great mysteries will be elusive no longer.

From the Big Bang to your essential role in creation... if you seek meaning to life in general, and your life in particular, you *absolutely, definitely* should read **the Fall**.

...Your views of spirituality, science, and reality are about to change forever.

'If I had to be on a desert island with only one book, this would be it.' James D'Angelo.

'The Fall is the most important spiritual book ever written.' Jean Whittle

'I have been on this journey for more than 40 years and this book just joins all the dots for me. It is astonishing. It is of vital importance, please read it.' Katydr (Amazon).

'Here are the answers to life's impossible contradictions, and what we can do for ourselves and others – brilliant!' Jan (Amazon).

'It is like the missing piece of the puzzle that I have been looking for!' Judy Moen.

'One of the most powerful and influential books in my entire life, completely altering my world view.' Peter De Ruyter.

ISBN: 978-1-906625-05-4

Available from good bookshops, Amazon or direct from thejosephcommunications.us
Also available as an e-Book and audiobook.

Also available in **The Joseph Communications** series:

Trance Mission

Over a period of three years Joseph was asked more than 150 questions 'live' by those attending twelve remarkable public trance demonstrations.

His illuminating, eloquent answers are reproduced word-for-word in this double-sized, 448-page book, in which Joseph focuses on and expands our understanding of a wide range of spiritual topics, including:

pre-destiny and choice • the nature of time • natural disasters • Indigo children • meditation techniques • God • the future of the planet • aliens • reincarnation • angels • past-life baggage • sexual energy • healing • the Bible • animals • infant mortality • ascension • the reason for accidents ...and many more.

As with each Joseph title, **Trance Mission**'s contents are shot through with his refreshingly no-nonsense approach to spirituality. Highly illuminating, deeply spiritual and presenting practical information on every page, **Trance Mission** also gives a unique insight into Joseph's background and relationship with his 'instrument' Michael, immersing all who read it in the unique, irresistible atmosphere of his public trance appearances.

'I can't say how satisfying it is to read someone's question that exactly mirrors my own, and what deep and thought-provoking answers Joseph provides.' Eugenie Heraty.

'It is such an extraordinary book - so many new perspectives on old ideas.' Peter Wallace.

'Rarely do you read any "channeled" material that answers questions directly and sensibly. This is the book that does and I highly recommend it to anyone on their spiritual journey.' Meria Heller.

'Wonderful - many of the additional questions I had been asking after reading the other four books have been answered.' Rowen Harris.

'Truly, it's fabulous! I'm finding it to be a real page-turner. I love it.' Ian Davison.

'Trance Mission is a magnificent read – so many answers to questions that spiritual truth-seekers yearn to know.' Joanna Eden.

'Anyone seeking to be uplifted from this negative world view should read Trance Mission – much Love and Light and hope on every page.' Christine Wood.

ISBN: 978-1-906625-06-1

Available from good bookshops, Amazon or direct from thejosephcommunications.us
Also available as an e-Book and audiobook.

Also available in **The Joseph Communications** series:

From Here to Infinity

...In this sixth book in the acclaimed series Joseph clarifies, demystifies and redefines – from a spiritual perspective – many of the major earthly concepts we take for granted and find ourselves immersed in including: Time, Space, Energy, Perception, Memory and Infinity.

Joseph also offers further insights into the nature of the Divine and, by exploring and enhancing our creative potential, he reveals advanced ways of transforming and elevating our inner and outer worlds and infusing our lives and the matrix of this entire planet with the highest expression of Light.

As a reader of the Joseph Communications, this 288-page volume is set to expand your ability to live in the Light and to give out the Light, offering new methods and meditations that will further empower you to make a real difference in this world by – literally – illuminating yourself, those around you, and the physical landscape you are currently a part of.

'Oh boy, Joseph really seems to have lifted the tempo this time.'
Kate Wrigglesworth.

'Joseph REALLY gets into the nuts and bolts of what's NEEDED for us Warriors of the Light! I'm so humbled by this information.'
Jorge Castaneda.

'I don't mind admitting that the last chapter moved me to tears. This book has made me more determined than ever to meditate daily to send Light out to the world.'
Tracy Dewick.

'I wish it were required reading in every school, library and institution, so important is the message.'
Jeannie Judd.

ISBN: 978-1-906625-08-5

Available from good bookshops, Amazon or direct from thejosephcommunications.us
Also available as an e-Book and audiobook.